THE STORY OF EDINBURGH CRYSTAL

1. Frontispiece

Jenkinson Venetian-style glass. H $11\frac{7}{8}''$
(Courtesy, Glasgow Museums and Art Galleries.)

THE STORY OF
EDINBURGH CRYSTAL

by

H W Woodward

Published by DEMA GLASS Limited

Printed by Blackwood Pillans & Wilson Limited, Leith Walk, Edinburgh

1984

CONTENTS

THE STORY OF EDINBURGH CRYSTAL

LIST OF ILLUSTRATIONS

INTRODUCTION

Heritage '84, promoted by the British Tourist Authority, seems an appropriate year in which to publish an account of an industry whose products during the past two centuries have been part of Scotland's proud heritage.

Here briefly is the story of glassmaking and glass decorating in the Edinburgh region, tracing in particular the progress of one firm now the sole survivor of the crystal glass manufacturers of the area, placing the firm in its historical context. In recent years Edinburgh Crystal has moved from antiquated premises to modern, well equipped works, using sophisticated furnaces and plant to meet the challenge of the present and the future, in design, making, and decorating. Maintenance of high quality in these fields is most critical to the firm's well-being. Even so, in the crafts of glassmaking and decorating, methods have remained basically the same through the centuries. These skills, now being practised by an encouraging number of younger people, are enhanced by peripheral technological improvements. It was thought desirable to record the story of the past, with an account of today's achievements, giving cause for both pride and optimism.

During the writing of this work great help has been received from a number of sources. The author wishes to thank the many members of the Edinburgh Crystal staff and workforce, past and present, who have assisted. As many of the firm's records have disappeared, this assistance has been invaluable. Particular thanks are due to those who have made an actual contribution to this history, and also to Mr E A Stott, Chairman, who read the manuscript and made helpful suggestions; and to Mr L England, Director Crystal Production, and Mr S R Eveson, ex-Works and Technical Director of Thomas Webb's, both of whom provided most of the technical information, thereby ensuring much more detail and accuracy.

A number of people not connected with the Firm have helped, and sincere thanks are also extended to them: Messrs H A Basterfield, B J R Blench, J Lawrie, T McCall, J O Nelson, R Newton, R Oddy, Mrs C R Sauvage, Miss S McDougall and Staff of Edinburgh Central Library, also Staffs of the National Library of Scotland, Royal Scottish Museum, and Huntly House Museum, Edinburgh, and the Museum and Art Gallery, Kelvingrove, Glasgow. The work involved has been a co-operative, enjoyable, and friendly effort.

H W W March 1984.

1. Early Days

Although neither Edinburgh nor Leith can rightfully claim to be the birthplace of Scottish glass, these towns certainly have the distinction of being the home, for three centuries, of its development and maturity. The period covering the early days of glass bottle making in Leith during the 17th century, to the production of finest quality crystal and coloured glass in Edinburgh during the 19th and 20th centuries, makes a fascinating and important chapter in the history of glass.

An early Scottish glass-making site was at East Wemyss in the Kingdom of Fife. King James VI of Scotland, later James I of England, in 1610 granted Sir George Hay (de Haye) of Nethercliff a patent or monopoly to make glass in Scotland for a period of 31 years. His manufactory was in the largest of nine caves on the southern Fife shore, a spot to become known as Glass Cove or Cave. Sir George, owner of ironworks at Letterewe, Wester Ross, during 1620 acquired the services of Venetian glass-makers. These men had worked under Sir Robert Mansell, the English monopolist, at the London Broad Street works, but had left because of labour troubles. Hay was in competition with Mansell but in 1627 he sold out to Thomas Robertson, a London merchant, acting on behalf of Mansell. In 1631 the East Wemyss Works closed and during the Civil War the patent lapsed. Later in the century attempts were made to revive the industry there, new coal mines being sunk nearby, but without success.

With primitive roads and transport it was essential that the source of raw materials needed for making glass should not be too distant. On the Fife coast, the main ingredient, sand, was plentiful; there was an abundance of the large sea-weed, kelp, which when burned provided potash. Sea shells when ground could be used as lime. In the early years there was a good supply of timber for firing furnaces to melt glass and when the use of wood as fuel for this purpose was prohibited, there was no shortage close by of the new fuel, coal.

It is not surprising that by the middle of the 17th century the glass industry had become established on the other side of the Firth of Forth, at Leith, and later at Portobello and Prestonpans. Here were the raw materials also, and importantly, a large local demand for bottles and drinking glasses needed for imported wine and locally-made whisky and ale. The English naturalist, John Ray, reported that "while travelling along the shore at

2. Leith from Easter(n) Road, after Paul Sandby, 1751, showing the first of the glass-house cones built on the shore (to the right of sailing ship). (Author's collection)

Prestonpans in August 1661, I saw glass being produced from a mixture of kelp, salt, and local sand, all calcined and melted in ovens."

In 1697 William Morrison of Prestonpans was licensed to manufacture "all manner of vials, drinking and werch glasses": he specialised in "hand-keiking (looking) glasses". The following year he patented an engine for grinding, polishing, and cutting looking-glass plates, and later evolved a silvering process for mirrors involving the use of tin-foil and mercury "dabbed with a hare's paw to assist contact, penetration, and amalgamation".

When Charles II returned to the throne in 1660 various patents were revived. The licence for making glass came into the hands of Charles Hay, grandson of Sir George who had previously enjoyed the privilege. Charles sold the licence to his mother and uncle, who in turn sold it to Robert Pape, who sank all his money into the building of a glass-works in the Citadel at Leith. Cromwell had constructed the Citadel, which had five bastions, as a defence against the Scots. After the Restoration the site was given to the Earl of Lauderdale who sold it to the Council of Edinburgh for £6,000. From that time the Citadel became a place of trade and industry.

On Christmas Eve, 1663, there appeared the following advertisement in the first newspaper printed in Scotland, "The Kingdom's Intelligencer": "A remarkable Advertisement to the Country and Strangers. That there is a Glass-house erected on the Citadel at Leith where all sorts and quantities are made at the prices following". "Wine glasses, beer glasses, quart bottels, pynt bottels, chopin bottels, and muskin or mutchkin bottels" are listed. The prices were given in Scots money and the products proclaimed "better stuff and stronger than is imported."

Trade was slow and merchants continued to import bottles, so much so that complaints were made. In 1664 the Privy Council issued an order: "Robert Pape, Master-Glassmaker, who occupied a portion of the Citadel for some years could produce satisfactorily all manner of glassware and that as there was a danger from foreign glass then being imported affecting its prosperity and even its existence, they forbad the public buying bottles other than those made locally".

Charles Hay, apparently still involved in glass, during 1682 set up another works where superior quality clear drinking glasses were made. A few years later Leith produced fine laboratory and chemists' glass-ware, mainly to satisfy local demand, including that of Edinburgh University, then "our Tounis Colledge". By 1700 the industry employed 120 glass-blowers alone.

Foreign competition continued to have an adverse effect. English and Dutch bottle manufacturers flooded the Scottish market with their products. It was reported that at one stage 2600 dozen bottles had been imported into

Montrose alone. The Privy Council's order forbidding the purchase of foreign bottles seems not to have had the desired result. The Council made another effort, this time empowering the Leith glass manufacturers to seize imported consignments and hand them over to the Crown.

Eventually the patent passed into the hands of five partners, of whom Sir James Stanfield was the most active. For a short period they are said to have imported glassmakers from Newcastle. By 1680 their works had become dilapidated: the following year the partnership was disbanded and Sir James, with Sir Robert Gordon, bought the works. They employed Alexander Ainslie, who in turn took in three partners to start the firm of Ainslie and Co. Foreign competition brought about the closure of the works during the 1720s. A new company in 1746 tried to revive the works, but soon afterwards the premises were burned down.

During the 1710s Henry Kalmeter, from Sweden, toured Scotland to report back to his country on the British mining industry. He wrote "A mile from Edenburg on the east side and to the sea is Lith. In the town is . . . the glassworck belonging to Mr Wechtman and Befour, where they only make bottles, which are very good and strong and are there sold for 20 pence a dozin. They take thereto ¾ parts of wood ashes, them they buy from London, ¼ of the refusals of the ashes of soap making, and as much sand as the ashes require. The seaware burnt, till it comes to a very hard body, and broken glass of bottels, is likewise mixed with it. This is all warmed in a furnace before they put it in the pots where it is smelted about 10 to 12 hours before they begin to draw the glass".

Before the middle of the 18th century Jacobite glasses began to appear.

Jacobite Glasses

No other glasses have such Scottish historical connotations as 18th century Jacobite glasses. The rather sad story of the Jacobite cause is reflected in these collectors' items which have remained highly desirable acquisitions since glass collecting began in modern times.

When Prince Charles Edward Stuart landed on the island of Eriskay in July, 1745, he and his followers began a rather forlorn attempt to restore his father to the British Throne. They were successful at first, occupying Perth and Edinburgh, and then achieving a convincing victory over Government forces at the Battle of Prestonpans in September, 1745. The triumphant march as far as Derby, the withdrawal back to Scotland, and the disaster at Culloden the following year, when the Stuart cause and the Highland clans received a blow from which they never recovered, is a well known story. During the 18th century, after the 1715 Rising, glasses were made for various Jacobite societies, firstly with obvious sentiments, but after Culloden, with hidden meanings. The origin of these glasses; where they

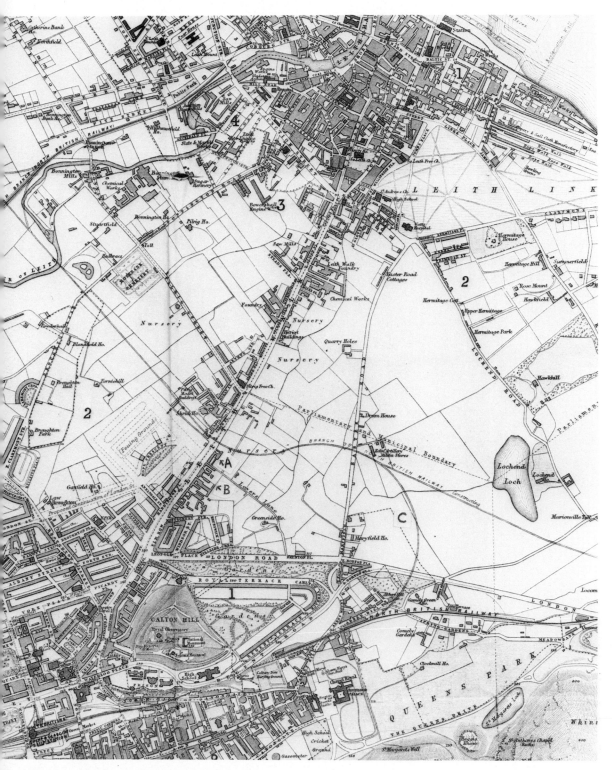

3. Hislop plan of Edinburgh, 1866: (A and B=37 and 33 Leith Walk; C=Norton Park). (Courtesy, Edinburgh Central Library)

4. Leith Walk in the 1840s, showing four of the seven glass-house cones in Leith. (Author's collection)

were made and who engraved them, has been a matter of conjecture, but some authorities give their birthplace as the Newcastle-upon-Tyne area. George Savage in his book *Glass* (1965) says of Jacobite glasses—"Most such glasses were made in Newcastle-on-Tyne and engraved (portrait glasses especially) in Edinburgh".

Naturally, most Jacobite glasses are those suitable for drinking toasts, but a few tumblers and decanters were produced. Wherever made or decorated, they play an important part in the establishment of glass engraving in the British Isles. In fact, it is no idle fancy to say that the engraving of the thistle motif on Edinburgh Crystal's Thistle service, is a continuation of the tradition which started in the 18th century with Jacobite glasses.

The early ones featured an engraved portrait of the Young Pretender, but after 1746 an actual portrait was replaced by something symbolic.

The first motif was the rose with one or two buds, representing the Crown of England to which, the Jacobites believed, the two Pretenders had a right. They were possibly represented by the buds. Other emblems were mainly a Thistle, and Oak Leaf (signifying Boscobel), and a Star. Less common were various flowers, and moths, grubs, and caterpillars, whose significance has not been satisfactorily determined. Latin mottoes were "Fiat" (Let it be done, i.e. drink to the Cause): "Floreat" (Will flourish again); "Radiat" (Star—the glory still shone): "Redeat" (May he come again): "Audentior Ibo" (with greater daring I will go)—or more likely "Audentior Bibo" (I drink more boldly). There was also the "Amen" glasses, on which verses from a Jacobite hymn were engraved (usually by diamond point) concluding with the word "Amen". Some Jacobite glasses had a coin enclosed in their stems.

Leith and Edinburgh glass companies

During this period came the birth of the most important of the Leith glass-works, a factory which survived for over a century. The chief partner in the new company, James Milne, decided in 1746 to rent part of Leith sands. Following the 1745 Jacobite rising, soldiers were stationed in Edinburgh Castle. There being a shortage of bricklayers, some of the soldiers were employed in building the first of the large glasshouse cones. Paul Sandby's "View of Leith" painted in 1751 shows this cone on the shore. In all seven cones were built and these were a dominating feature of the Leith shore sky-line until the early part of the twentieth century. A number of other views show these cones.★

★ *Portrait of William Inglis—Captain of Muirfield Golf Club, by David Allan. 1782.*
Edinburgh and Leith and surrounding country as seen from Calton Hill. Lithograph by J W Townsend. 1841.
Painting of Leith Sands Races, by Willie Reid. c. 1855.

In 1751 another company, the Edinburgh Glasshouse Company, feued land adjoining, and the second cone was erected. By 1772 the two firms, the Leith, and the Edinburgh Glass Companies were producing nearly 16,000 cwts. of bottles a year, and in 1788 the Leith company built a second bottle-works. This period was the heyday of bottle-making in Leith. During this era the Leith Company had its own armed ships for protection against pirates, especially those from the Netherlands.

During the 1790s there were six glassworks in Leith, making not only bottles in vast quantities, but, so the first Statistical Account of Scotland, published in 1791, claimed "as fine crystal and window glass . . . as anywhere in Europe". Even allowing for the superlatives of the times, it is evident that quality glass was being produced. With the dramatic increase in the drinking of wine, especially claret, and the decrease in ale consumption, there was a growing demand for better quality drinking glasses.

In the whole of Scotland, during the 30 years preceding 1790, glass manufactures rose from 1,769,712 lbs, to 9,059,904 lbs—a truly remarkable increase.

Writing in 1792 a contributor to "The Bee", an old Edinburgh periodical, commented that about 30 years before there had been only one glass company in Scotland, the hands working one-half the year in Glasgow, and the other half in Leith.

"Now there are six glass-houses in Leith alone, besides many others in different parts of the country. At the time I mention nothing else than bottles of coarse green glass were made there, and to that article the Glass House Company in Leith confined their efforts, till about a dozen years ago, when they began to make fine glass for phials and other articles of that nature. About four years ago they introduced the manufacture of crown** glass for windows, which they now make in great perfection, and in considerable quantities. After they began to manufacture white glass, they fell into the way of cutting it or ornament and engraving upon it. In this last department they have reached a higher degree of perfection that it has perhaps anywhere else ever attained. A young man who was bred to that business, having discovered a taste in designing, and an elegance of execution which was very uncommon, the proprietors of the works were at pains to give him every aid

---

**Crown glass was made as follows: In one method a bubble of molten glass was blown, flattened on a marver, and a pontil rod fixed opposite the blow iron. The blow iron was broken off, leaving a small hole, and in front of a "flashing" furnace the glass was spun rapidly on the punty until it "flashed"—opening out into a flat disc, three or four feet in diameter. The punty was then knocked off, leaving a punty mark—the bull's eye or bullion, reproduced on modern window glass imitating crown glass. There was an art in cutting the disc into suitably sized panes, with as little waste as possible, which could be used as cullet (glass melted with raw ingredients used to make glass). The marked piece in the centre was left as small as possible, to be used as cullet, or in skylights and poorer dwellings. Crown glass had a natural fire polish, and with a more brilliant surface was considered superior to "broad" or "slit-cylinder" glass.

in the art of drawing that this place can afford, and he has exhibited some specimens of his powers in that line that are believed to be unrivalled. It is but yesterday that this Glass House Company (who are in a very flourishing state) encouraged by their success in other respects, introduced the art of preparing glass in imitation of gems, and of cutting it into facets, and working it into elegant forms for chandeliers and other ornamental kinds of furniture. In this department their first attempts have been highly successful, and they have now executed some pieces of work that they need not be ashamed to compare with the best that can be procured elsewhere."

The works of the Glass House Company at Leith were offered for sale in the "Edinburgh Evening Courant" of 1813, the notice stating that the works were valued at £40,000 with "A valuable steam-engine of sixteen horse-power valued at £21,000".

Not only was Leith famous for the quantity and quality of its bottles, the works were noted for the skill of some of its glass-blowers in blowing bottles or carboys of tremendous size. One such bottle was "equal to the size of fully more than a hogshead".

Prior to 1804 directories record the glassworks in Leith separately as the Leith, or the Edinburgh Company glass-houses, on the Links, or in Baltic Street. For the next few years other works are listed in Kirkgate, Little Carron, and Elbe.

A famous name connected with the Edinburgh Glass House sited on The Links at Leith during the last decade of the 18th century and the first of the 19th was that of Archibald Geddes. Geddes became Resident Manager, and when a letter was submitted to the Committee for the Glass Trade approving the method of levying duties on "glass in the Annealing or Tempering Oven" rather than on "Materials or Metal in the Pott" it was he who signed "For the Glass Manufacturers of Scotland". This was during the period of the first tax on glass, short-lived because of effective opposition.

Then, in 1817, is recorded the Leith Bottle House with the most famous address of all. Salamander Street, Leith, was constructed after the completion of the new docks, and seems to have derived its name from the fiery furnaces within the works and the creature fabled to live in fire.

Just before 1825 the two companies amalgamated to become the Edinburgh and Leith Glass House Company, changing its title in 1833 to "Edinburgh and Leith Glass Company".

The New Statistical Account of Scotland (1845) mentions that although the seven glass-house cones were still standing, with 80 to 90 people employed in the works, they were producing only bottles. The hope was expressed "now that the excise duty has been repealed (referring to the second tax on glass from 1745 to 1845) and all fiscal restrictions removed, that the other branches of glass-manufacture, viz. plate-glass, window-glass, and crystal will be immediately resumed, and that these old and celebrated works will again present the enlivening bustle and stir of former days, when every cone was in operation".

Unfortunately the hope was not realised. Although Leith was to continue as a major sea–port and commercial centre, playing an essential part in Edinburgh's development, its glass trade suffered a steady decline. By 1850 only two of the seven Salamander Street cones were working. Bottles were made by the Edinburgh and Leith Glass Company until the 1870s, when the works closed down. In 1912 the last of the cones was demolished, thus finally removing a material monument to the great Leith industry. Leith, a town of great historic interest and commercial importance, after enjoying civic independence for almost a century, became absorbed in a new Edinburgh in 1920. But the proud spirit amongst older Leithers still remains.

Portobello

Portobello, now a popular seaside resort within the Edinburgh District Council's boundaries, lies just over two miles north east of the city centre. Glass-making began there in the late 1820s, within fifteen acres of land bounded by the Figgate Burn, the Dalkeith Road and the Fishwives Causeway, part of the Abercorn Estate known as "Adams Law".

Towards the end of the 18th century, chemical and brick works had been established, the chemical works producing amongst other things sulphuric acid. During the 1820s, Joseph Astley owned these: they were known as "The Secret Works".

Around 1829 the works were taken over by William Bailey. Bailey had been involved in the Newcastle glass trade, and during the 1820s was established at the Midlothian glass works in South Back of Canongate, Edinburgh. Wm. Bailey and Co. also had a retail warehouse for glass and china at 2 St. Andrew Square, and later at 25 Greenside Place. On the chemical works site the manufacture of flint and cut crystal glass began. Bailey's chief clerk was John Ford, who was later to develop the famous Holyrood glassworks. For a time there was a big demand for tumblers, decanters, and other table glass, but the firm suffered increasing competition from the Edinburgh and Leith glass trade, and in 1848 the works turned over to the more profitable production of green bottles, meeting the needs of the local wine, beer and whisky trade. William Bailey built himself a house which he called "Baileyfield", and the house later became the company's offices. The name remains today, commemorating one of Portobello's greatest benefactors.

In 1833, Bailey became the town's first Provost and from 1846 to 1848 served a second term of office. Meanwhile his firm became "Glass Manufacturers and Potters to Her Majesty", and his manufactory "Mid Lothian Glass Works".

About 1856, Richard Cooper from Staffordshire, joined the firm, whose name changed to "Bailey and Cooper". In 1859 William Bailey died. Cooper was then joined by his brother-in-law, Thomas Wood, also from a large Staffordshire flint-glass works, and the firm's name changed again to "Cooper and Wood".

In 1866, there seems to have been some disagreement; the partners separated, Cooper retaining the old works and Wood building new works around the Baileyfield House. Wood also was a public figure, becoming Provost of Portobello in 1867 for three years, and again in 1891 for a similar period. He travelled extensively in Germany and Sweden, later introducing improved methods in bottle-making learned during his visits, and brought over bottle-makers from those countries. Fifty bottle-makers arrived at Granton in 1885—half for Portobello and the remainder for Alloa.

Cooper adopted similar means of improving bottle production, but his works closed down during the 1926 general strike and never re-opened.

The Wood's works survived, firstly under the umbrella of the Distillers Company and then The United Glass Bottle Manufacturers, until January 1968 when, with the closing down of these works, Portobello lost an industry which had brought some fame and wealth to the district for over a century and a half.

(For further details see "United Glass in Scotland: 2. The Portobello Works" by HA Basterfield in "Scottish Goodware", June 1966).

Edinburgh

Few cities can equal the scenic splendour of Edinburgh, "the Athens of the North", with its view of the Castle across Princes Street Gardens. It was Sir Walter Scott's "mine own romantic town", Robert Fergusson referring to Edinburgh in one of his poems as "Auld Reikie (Reekie)". The Castle, on its rock (one of Edinburgh's ancient volcanos) is an important factor in the history of Scotland's capital. This fortress in troublous times during the 12th century was regarded as a safe place of residence for Scotland's sovereign and retinue. After the City lost its regal and parliamentary importance following the country's union with England, Edinburgh, in spite of civil strife and foreign invasion, had become an important centre for law, literature, religion, commerce and education, with its famous University founded in 1583. Although industry has not been the main feature of Edinburgh's development, the city and the port of Leith have not lacked a wide variety of industries and trades connected with printing and publishing, shipping, brewing, distilling, rubber products, electronics, coal, cloth and clothing, and pottery and glass.

The decline of the glass trade in Leith and Portobello was due partly to the rise of Edinburgh as an important glass centre. A manufactory known as the Caledonian Glassworks operated in the North Back of Canongate (now Calton Road) at the end of the 18th century. These works were bought in 1810 by William Ford; five years later he transferred the works to Bull's Close, off the South Back Canongate. In 1813 William died, his nephew John Ford forming a new company, which was dissolved in 1835, when another company was formed in its place. Fine quality glass was being made, John Ford becoming Flint Glass Manufacturer to Queen Victoria during the first year of her reign in 1837. Apart from crystal glass for the table, a wide range of decorative ware was also developed.

A large epergne in the Huntly House Museum vividly portrays the skills of Ford's glass-makers and decorators. This wonderful specimen was on display at the Edinburgh Exhibition of 1886 and was later used for at least one state banquet at Holyroodhouse. Another Ford production was a range of goblets with a coin enclosed in the hollow part of the stem. These were very popular at the time of Queen Victoria's Golden Jubilee. More unusual, during the 1840s, paperweights and bottles featured sulphides, or cameo incrustations inside, notably portrait heads of famous people such as Shakespeare and Sir Walter Scott. These "cameos" were in opaque white after the style of the French paperweights and those of Apsley Pellatt in London. Some of the finest of all Ford products were the copper-wheel engraved items, ranging from glasses for the nobility decorated with their coats-of-arms, embellished with gilding, to less expensive but none the less beautiful pieces. The engraving often had Grecian and other classical designs. Bremner (1869) mentions a small jug engraved with amazing minuteness showing one of the Elgin Marbles friezes. According to Bremner, the firm's engraving had developed from "the coarse and inartistic work" shown in the 1856 Edinburgh Art Exhibition, to the specimens displayed in the London International Exhibition of 1862, which had received favourable comment from the art critics, culminating in the magnificent show at the Paris Exhibition of 1878. Famous engravers who did work for Ford's were the Millers (Mullers) of Bohemian origin, and John Smith, of Bangor Road, Leith. Bremner also comments on the firm's wine glasses, the rims and feet having a small amount of colour "not like the heavy appearance of uniform coloured Bohemian glass". As a contrast were some large decanters, which brought forth "the admiration of the French for the bibulous capacity of the Scotch for the chief wine of France".

One of Ford's later productions on a larger scale was a range of high quality tableware, featuring cut fluted hollow stems and cut fluted hollow stoppers. Glasses engraved with the popular fern motif became another well known Ford feature. A writer in "The Scotsman" of August 8, 1866 describes a visit to the Holyrood Glass Works, "by far the most extensive and complete manufacturing and cutting works of any in this quarter. Upwards of two hundred hands are employed in them". After describing the materials and methods used in glass making, the writer states "The glassmakers are engaged every alternative six hours from Monday to Friday, working regular hours, but sometimes nearly eighteen hours in twenty-four when working extra time. It is difficult to ascertain the wages of a glassmaker, seeing so much depends on the ability and steadiness of the man, and of the description of the work engaged at. At ordinary and every-day work, a good hand can make £2 a week and often more. What may be termed fabulous wages are occasionally made." Hence to the cutting department. "Here every description of table and ornamental crystal and glass for general purposes is manufactured and cut . . . All shades of colour are to be seen, with endless varieties of new and old patterns made from designs kept on the premises, or from models brought by customers. The glass-cutter, like the glass-maker, will turn out copies of any design submitted to him, depending little on pencil, but greatly on his wheel, keen eye, and steady hand. It would be difficult to say whether the cut or engraved glass was most worthy of admiration . . . Representations of foliage, flowers, fruit, heraldry, architectural edifices, and of animals meet the eye." A glass goblet with a small silver coin in the stem is described. Glass-cutters' wages averaged 34 shillings a week.

In recognition of their work in producing for the Royal Family a number of goblets and christening mugs engraved with views of Balmoral Castle, the firm was allowed to re-name its works "The Royal Holyrood Glass-Works". The change of title in 1898 was an honour unfortunately short-lived, the works closing down in 1904. Many of the Ford craftsmen joined the Edinburgh and Leith Flint Glass-Works at Norton Park, about which we shall read more later. It should be remembered that the decorators at least had to be skilled in things other than glass: they were competent engineers and wood turners. In those days the mild steel wheels used in cutting glass, and the wooden wheels for polishing, had to be regularly re-shaped. These varied skills they passed on to the workers at Norton Park.

In Holyrood Road, the present name for South Back of Canongate, are some tenements, incorporated in the frontage of which are two plaques, one depicting a glass-blower at work, and the other a glass-cutter. These are the last reminders of the most famous of Edinburgh's nineteenth century glass-works. The tenements may be demolished to make way for a brewery extension, but it is understood that the plaques will be preserved in any new frontage.

Bremner, writing of the later 1860s, gives interesting details of the other aspects of glass manufactures. Mentioning that Ford employed 200 persons, he goes on to reveal that glass-makers earned from 20 shillings to 38 shillings per week. (The wages varied according to whether they were at weekly or piece-work rates, but averaged 34 shillings). Cutters received 20 shillings to 34 shillings; engravers 20 shillings to 40 shillings; and boys 4 shillings to 5 shillings. Trade Union activities were fairly advanced for the time. Entry money into the National Flint-Glass Makers' Sick and Friendly Society of Great Britain and Ireland was from 10 shillings to £7, with contributions up to 10 pence weekly. Weekly sick pay for 13 weeks was 12 shillings, reducing to 5 shillings. Members on strike were allowed 15 shillings per week for six months. Any member wishing to emigrate was paid from £8 to £10. Retirement superannuation amounted to 3 shillings to 8 shillings weekly, depending upon how long the pensioner had been a member. There is a slightly modern note about the statement "that the Union does not permit employment of more than one apprentice to five journeymen (except in special circumstances). Employers in want of a workman must apply through the Union District Secretary". Glass-cutters had a separate Union at that time.

The Edinburgh and Leith Branches of both the Glass-Makers' and Glass Cutter's Societies were early members of the Edinburgh and District Trades Council. They joined in April 1859 but ten years later "owing to the great difficulty in which the (glass) trade was placed with regard to the attendance of their delegates they had been obliged to withdraw from the Council altogether".

5. Jenkinson's glass and china warehouse in Princes Street. (Author's collection)

— 15 —

6. Jenkinson Venetian-style glass. H 6⅞″ (Courtesy, Glasgow Museums and Art Galleries)

7. Jenkinson Venetian-style glass. (Courtesy, Royal Scottish Museum, Edinburgh)

8. Jenkinson Venetian-style glass, *c.* 1880. (Courtesy, Royal Scottish Museum, Edinburgh)

2. Leith Walk

There is now only one survivor of the old Edinburgh glass manufacturers: the Edinburgh Crystal Glass Co., a firm with a history spanning more than a century. For most of the century its works was actually in Edinburgh, at first in the Edinburgh part of Leith Walk. This thoroughfare is of more than usual historic interest. The Walk, or Loan, was originally a parapet with a trench below, constructed by the Scottish Covenanters. Such was their spirit that even "ladies of honour" amongst them helped in raising the earthwork, stretching from the redoubt at Leith and St. Anthony's Port, to the one at Calton Hill. These armed redoubts covered the open ground towards Restalrig, and entrenched behind these defences, the Scottish Army under their General, Sir Alexander Leslie, was able to repel the Cromwellian attacks from the east. When peace came the embankment became a walk. It is probable that most of the soil forming the embankment was returned to fill up the trenches, and that the walk at its present level was constructed at a later period. In 1748 Defoe described it as a "handsome gravel walk, twenty feet broad, and no horses suffered to come upon it". With the opening of North Bridge in 1772 the Walk became a carriage road, and by the 1820s had become what Sir Daniel Wilson described as being "converted at great expense into one of the broadest and most substantial causeways in the Kingdom, along which handsome streets and squares are now laid out, uniting the capital and its seaport into one great city". A popular recreation among Edinburgh residents and others was an evening stroll along the Walk, culminating in a meal of Leith's famous Forth oysters.

At the foot of Calton Hill, leading to Leith Walk proper, were Greenside Lane, Greenside Place, Baxter Place, and Picardy Place, the homes of glass-makers, cutters, and engravers. Number 17 Leith Walk was the home and workplace of the first of the Millers, the Bohemian engravers already mentioned. The first glassworks to be established in Leith Walk was that of John Ranken and Co. Beginning about 1798 as a "Glass warehouse" situated at "middle Leith Walk, east side", within a few years flint glass was being manufactured, the address recorded in the Edinburgh directories as "37 Leith Walk". The works was situated on the corner of Lovers Lane or Loan. The whole of Leith Walk has now been re-numbered, with the romantically named thoroughfare replaced by a more prosaic Brunswick Road and other streets leading into London Road and Easter Road. The works closed down during the 1830s but was re-opened in the next decade by Thomas and Fraser at 38 Leith Walk. At that time no. 37 was occupied by a school slate manufacturer. The works became known as the Edinburgh Flint Glass Works, being noted as such in the Ordnance Survey map published in 1853.

Donald Fraser had previously worked at 18 Picardy Place as a glass-stainer, decorator and engraver. The works expanded and became 37 and 38 Leith Walk, but around the year 1860, when it was known that the site would be required shortly for the building of a railway goods station, Fraser's partner, John Thomas, moved to 33 Leith Walk, previously used as a dairy by the Douglas family. Fraser stayed at 37 and 38 until 1864, when he moved his business to 5 Baxter Place, and then York Lane. At Bathgate he converted the Old Brewery there into the West Lothian Flint Glass Works, operating the works from 1866 until his death in 1869. It survived until 1887 under the ownership of Wilson and Son, Glasgow, and then James Couper and Sons, also of Glasgow, well known for their "Clutha" glass.

At the time of the move John Thomas must have known that 33 Leith Walk would have to make way for mainly residential development in the area. However, he died on 7th October 1864. The works at 33 Leith Walk continued under the management of executors who were required to carry on the business if expedient for five years, and then dispose of it to the best advantage for the benefit of the four Thomas daughters. One of the daughters, Margaret, had married someone who became John Thomas Junior, either having originally the same name as his father-in-law by coincidence, or adopting it for business reasons. He was one of the executors. After the five years had elapsed it is not clear whether the works was sold, but before the period ended the works was listed in the 1867/68 Edinburgh Directory as being under the ownership of the Edinburgh and Leith Flint Glass Co. (not to be confused with the Edinburgh and Leith Glass Co., of 6 Salamander Street, Leith).

By 1873 Alexander Jenkinson had become associated with 33 Leith Walk. He was born on 5th May 1821, son of an East Lothian shepherd. His mother was Alison Grieve. Alexander's brothers, William and James, became East Lothian farmers and, during the 1840s, partners in a wines and spirits business at Kirkgate, Leith. Another brother, Maitland, ran a similar enterprise in Cable Wynd. About 1860 Alexander joined the firm of John Miller and Co., 21 Leith Street and 2 South St. Andrew Street, Edinburgh. Miller was potter to Her Majesty, and a china, pottery, and glass merchant. In 1867 Miller and Jenkinson signed a five year agreement in which the former subscribed £4000 and the latter £2000. Miller controlled the buying side and Jenkinson the selling. When the agreement expired in 1872 Jenkinson became established as a China Pottery and Glass Merchant in his own right at no. 10 Princes Street and soon afterwards as a glass manufacturer at 33 Leith Walk. Brother William, who died in 1878 when only 28 years of age, was also involved in the Princes Street business. Number 10 was one of the first buildings to be erected in the best known of Edinburgh's New Town streets. An earlier occupant, from 1823 to 1826, was Archibald Constable, whose firm issued the works of Scotland's most famous author, Sir Walter Scott. Scott was financially involved in the firm and was partner in James Ballantyne's printing business. When the crash came in 1826, the bankruptcy of both firms caused him personal ruin. The following year saw a sale of books at no. 10, part of Constable's sequestrated estate. Afterwards the premises were used variously by a carver and gilder, a stationer, a jeweller, and a wines and spirits merchant.

Alexander Jenkinson was not only a leading businessman, but was also foremost in an important part of Edinburgh's religious life. He played an active role in Sunday School and mission work. James Gall, Junior, son of the well known printer of Gall and Inglis fame, paid a deserved tribute to him in his "Carrubbers Close Mission: its planting and first fruits" published by Gall and Inglis in 1860. Gall writes: "The accession of Mr Jenkinson to our ranks, with his class of young women, imported additional life to our mission, and helped very much to shape the course it was to pursue. Having accepted the superintendance of the Sabbath morning school, he found most important employment for the young women of his evening class, by setting them to teach the little children, while they themselves also received lessons in teaching." The Carrubbers Close Mission still flourishes in the High Street as a Christian Centre.

The Jenkinson firm manufactured plain wine glasses, decanters with cut decoration, and other types of crystal glass, for sale to London firms including Thos. Goode, Harrods, and Army and Navy Stores.

Writing in the ART JOURNAL of 1875, Professor Archer, Director of the Edinburgh Museum then known as the Museum of Science and Art, describes a visit to "Mr A Jenkinson's Leith Walk Glass Works, Edinburgh". "For a long time past Edinburgh has been advancing rapidly in the manufacture of the finer kinds of table-glass, and in glass engraving. In the Exhibition of 1862 the ornamental glass of Edinburgh attracted considerable attention: and in the Paris Exhibition of 1867 the French reporters of the jury wrote in terms of great praise of the engraving and exquisite clearness of the material in the specimens of ornamental flint-glass from Edinburgh. Whether any immediate pecuniary benefit arose to the Scottish exhibitors upon the two occasions referred to is not known, but it is quite certain that the admiration excited by their productions has had a great effect in stimulating both masters and artisans, and causing a very considerable development of the manufacture both in Edinburgh and Glasgow. At the works named above there is a large number of processes, and as great a variety of products, as can be found in any glass works in the kingdom; and some of the operatives possess such remarkable skill and intelligence, that, were it not for the constant demand upon their time in the production of the staple articles of manufacture, they would certainly produce much of novelty and excellence. They work in *reticella* (a form of decoration in which fine threads of white or coloured glass are embedded in clear glass criss-crossing to form a filigree network), in moulding and pinching, in jewelling and floral ornamentation: and indeed in nearly all the processes of the Venetian glass workers with such skill, that it is not too much to hope the time is not far distant when, if not rivals, they will be no mean competitors with their brother workmen in Murano. In one thing they excel all continental artists, and that is in the exquisite purity of the material: water itself is not more clear and transparent, but this entails weight, and precludes all hope of attaining that almost aerial lightness, combined with strength, which makes the Venetian glass unique. Moreover, our home artists in this most beautiful of materials have to learn that wonderful power of creating new forms while still the lump of glass is hanging molten at the end of their blowpipes: the Venetians breathe their fancies into it, and the most wonderful and beautiful shapes issue from it with magical quickness. There is, however, amongst the Edinburgh glass-workers a most earnest love of their art and an anxious desire to advance it; and, more than any other class of artisans in the locality, they avail themselves of the opportunities for study which are afforded them by the extensive collections of ancient and modern examples in the Museum of Science and Art, where there are excellent examples of Roman glasswork, beside the large collection of old Venetian made by Abbate Sannetti, Director of the Museum of Murano; with selections of Bohemian, French, German, Russian, and English, from the various Exhibitions which have been held for the last fifteen years; and it is satisfactory to be able to record that the Saturday half-holiday is looked upon as a much-prized means of studying these examples by the better class of workmen of Scotland".

Immediately prior to this account, the Company extended its works to include the premises adjoining no. 34 Leith Walk, but apparently this was not enough, for during the year following the report, a move was made to Norton Park, and this was to be the Company's home for almost a century.

For a more detailed account of the Jenkinson family see notes by Mr H A Basterfield deposited in the Edinburgh Room of Edinburgh Central Library.

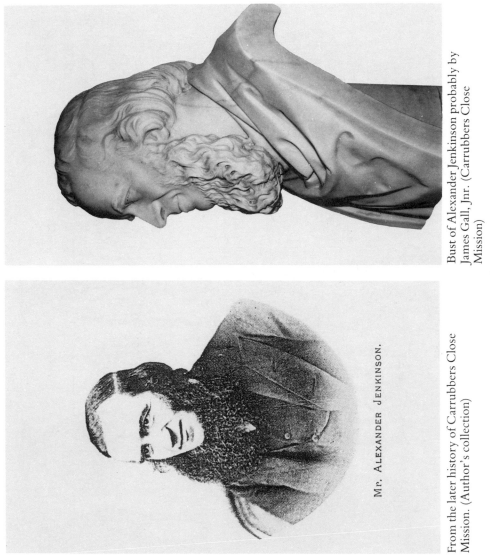

Mr. Alexander Jenkinson.

From the later history of Carrubbers Close Mission. (Author's collection)

Bust of Alexander Jenkinson probably by James Gall, Jnr. (Carrubbers Close Mission)

8a

PARIS INTERNATIONAL EXHIBITION.

151

We engrave some of the contributions of Messrs. JENKINSON & Co., of Edinburgh: they are of engraved glass, and have been placed by all critics among the best works of the class that have been sent by Great Britain in competition with the hitherto unrivalled fabricants of Germany and France. Messrs. Jenkinson take rank as one of those enterprising firms that maintain British supremacy in a class of Art in which not many years ago we admitted inferiority. They are a credit to Scotland.

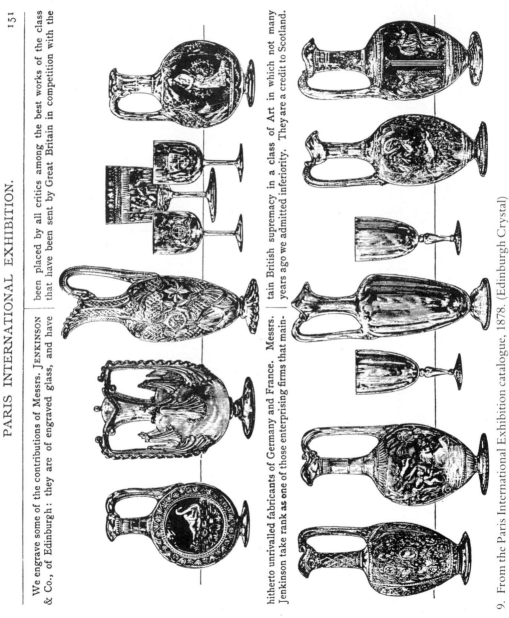

9. From the Paris International Exhibition catalogue, 1878. (Edinburgh Crystal)

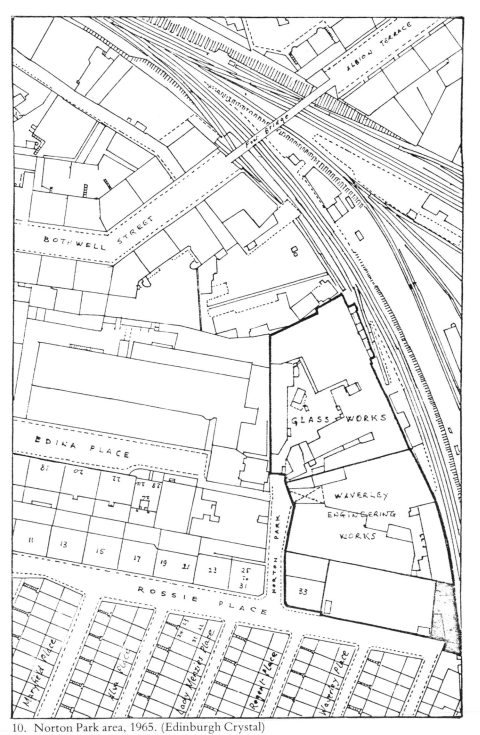

10. Norton Park area, 1965. (Edinburgh Crystal)

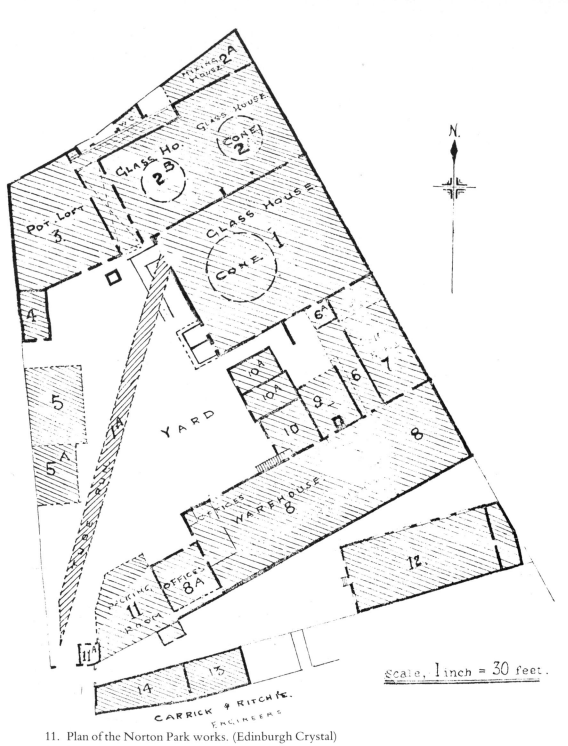

11. Plan of the Norton Park works. (Edinburgh Crystal)

1 *The prepared clay is put through the "pugging" machine, which compresses it.* 2 *Laying the pot bottom.* 3 *The sides of the pot are carefully built up.* 4 *The domed roof is shaped.* 5 *Finishing off the dipping hole.* 6, 7 *and* 8 *The heated pot is set into the furnace.*

12. Pot making and setting at Norton Park. (Edinburgh Crystal)

3. Norton Park

Norton Park is simply a narrow thoroughfare, with access from Easter Road or London Road, less than a mile to the south east of the old works in Leith Walk. Farmland and nursery gardens a few years before had become a rapidly developing district of houses and works. Until Leith Walk was converted into a carriage road early in the nineteenth century, Easter (or Eastern) Road was the main road linking Edinburgh from Canongate, Water Gate, and Abbey Hill, to Leith. The new glassworks, with a 12 pot furnace, was built at the side of the loop of the Edinburgh, Leith and Granton Branch of the North British Railway, just north of Abbey Hill Station. The section of Easter Road leading for a short distance from London Road was known as The Mall, then Maryfield—hence the various address names of the new works—Norton Park, Abbey Hill, Easter Road, London Road, and Maryfield, all for the same location. Happily, although most of the early business records of the firm have disappeared, the most important, the pattern books, dating from 1870s, have largely survived. This invaluable source of information makes it obvious that as soon as the firm settled at Norton Park, more ambitious products began to appear. For instance, crystal glass was decorated not only by cutting and engraving, but by other techniques such as "crackling" and "threading". Fine quality Venetian style glass was further developed. A notable production was glasses with fine "straw" stems, and also delicately blown items known as "muslin" or "mousseline". By 1878 the firm felt confident enough to put on show its table and fancy glass at the Paris Universal Exhibition. A writer in the official exhibition catalogue praised their engraved glass which "had been placed by all critics amongst the best works of the class that have been sent by Great Britain in competition with the hitherto unrivalled fabrications of Germany and France. They are a credit to Scotland".

However, Joseph Leicester reporting on the exhibits of Jenkinson of Edinburgh pays his firm a rather back-handed compliment. "Here is marvellous work, showing qualities of manipulation capable of accomplishing anything worthy of being done; yet nearly all their products are imitations. Why is this? Are we so poor in design that a field cannot be found for things which are decisive and original? In this stall one designer appears to me to have been inured by a wrong use of this power of imitation. If imitation may be taken to imply flattery, then assuredly the Venetians are flattered by this firm. I could not help a sigh as I looked over this beautiful

13. Glass–house at Norton Park, 1950s. (Courtesy, Scotsman Publications)

work: what could the same hands have done had they sought a purer style, and entered upon a freer course? Nothing can be more glorious and beautiful than the Grecian development, nothing more unlike it than the stale wearisome repetitions and imitations in modern times. The Greek productions themselves have a living power to this day, but all their imitations are cold and tiresome. The old Greeks made beautiful things because they did not imitate . . . One gets tired of this constant repetition of a Venetian goblet, a Venetian jug, as if nothing else in the world could be made . . . Let us hope that this firm will find out a purer field of activity than the Venetian. The faults chiefly observed are the want of truer conceptions of soft subdued colour, purity of form, and lightness of material. Their goblet of 7oz weight, capable of holding five or six quarts, is itself a marvel of manipulative skill, and deserving of a medal. It clearly shows what its makers could have accomplished in other walks of artistic manufacture."

14. Cutting shop at Norton Park, 1951. (On the left can be seen two of the Ballantine square decanters). (Courtesy, Scotsman Publications)

Not everyone would agree with the writer's criticism of Jenkinson's "a la façon de Venise". The Venetians were outstanding glass producers, responsible for the revival of glass-making soon after the Renaissance, creating a fashion in glass-making and decoration which dominated European glass for much of the 16th and 17th centuries. It seemed natural that glass-makers should emulate the best of Venetian glass, especially as there was a revival in the demand for Venetian-style glass, a demand met by such firms as Salviati.

One Jenkinson pattern book certainly included drawings of some very ornate glass of this type. It is possible that Jenkinson imported glass-makers from Italy, but whoever was responsible, the glass they produced would have been a credit to the craftsmen of any country.

Fortunately, there are examples of the Venetian-style "made in Edinburgh" glass in the Art Gallery and Museum, Kelvingrove, Glasgow

15. Part of the Royal Infirmary procession, *c.* 1926. (Courtesy, Mr George Gay)

(the Museum having the foresight to buy a collection from Jenkinson in 1876), and in the Royal Scottish Museum, Edinburgh.

Alexander Jenkinson died on 11th January 1880. He lies buried in Rosebank Cemetery, Pilrig Street, with other members of his family and near the graves of some ancestors. A moving tribute to him is paid in a later history of the Carrubbers Mission, covering the years 1858 to 1909, entitled "These Fifty Years". "A very heavy loss was sustained by the Mission in January 1880, when Mr Alex Jenkinson, who for more than twenty years had been its strength and sinew, was called to his rest. Mr Gall, his friend and comrade-in-arms, wrote of him: "Edinburgh does not, and cannot, know the loss which it has sustained in the death of our beloved brother; only those who have been associated with him during the last twenty years, and have seen his works and charity, and service and faith, and his patience, and his last works more than his first, can rightly appreciate the value of the man, or estimate the loss which the cause of Christ has sustained, not only in Edinburgh but in the world at large. They would say, in the language of David when he mourned over Abner, 'Know ye not that there is a prince and a great man fallen this day in Israel?' Other men have occupied far more distinguished places in society and the Church than he, but we venture to affirm that for many years he was the most truly valuable man which the City of Edinburgh possessed."

Alexander Jenkinson left personal estate amounting to almost £10,000 including stock worth £6340 at Princes Street and £1320 at Norton Park. He bequeathed £300 to Carrubbers Close Mission and a sum to ensure an annual income of £500 for his widow.

The business was continued by his son, Alexander Dixson Jenkinson born on 14th October 1853, and therefore aged 26 years at the time of his father's death.

During the 1880s the company began to develop lighting ware to meet the huge demand for both gas and electric light shades. This ware included "moons" and "globes", a utility line decorated by cutting, engraving, etching, and obscuring, using solid and stained colours. (In obscuring, a glass article was fixed to a lathe and the surface dulled by using a wire brush fed by sand and water—a not very skilled or well-paid job.)

Alongside this branch of glass manufacture matured the type of glass for which the Edinburgh and Leith Flint Glass Co. became world famous—cut and engraved crystal (or flint) glass. Crystal glass got its name from the natural silicate crystal, regarded as a semi-precious stone, found in the earth's surface, and known as rock crystal, which glass-makers tried to emulate, as they did natural coloured crystals. "Flint" glass is so called because glass was once made from silica "flints" or pebbles, ground and calcined before being finally melted with soda, lime, or potash, to make glass. (Clear glass is referred to in the trade as "flint"—meaning a colourless, rather than a *type* of glass.) For two or three centuries sand has been used instead of "flints", but the name remains.

Edinburgh craftsmen produced crystal glass skilfully decorated with intricate cut patterns, reminiscent of America's "Brilliant" period, and equalling any British cut glass hitherto. Their engraving also reached a very high standard. The normal engraving was (and still is) done by copper wheels varying from the size of a pin-head to about four inches in diameter, the wheels being fed with emery powder and oil, with the decoration dull or matt just as the glass leaves the wheel. Engraved decoration of this type was therefore distinct from the background and any other form of decoration, especially cutting which had been polished and remained secondary to the engraving. During the 1880s, however, a new technique was introduced. The engraved portions were polished and, combined with the polished background and cut patterns, became more of an integral part of the glass article itself. This became known as "Rock Crystal". The early manufactured Rock Crystal began with deeply cut pillared glass, and polished engraving added. In the polishing processes mentioned, wood, lead, and

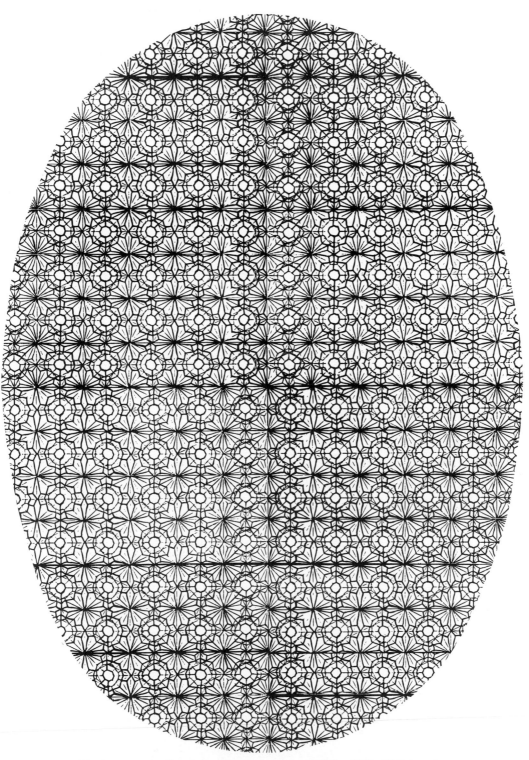

16. Large oval toilet tray, richly cut pattern (B785) *c.* 1886. (Edinburgh Crystal)

brush wheels were used, together with various powders, including putty powder and pumice. Undoubtedly the inspiration came from the work of the old lapidaries using the natural rock crystal.

In the firm's records pattern C10½ is referred to as a service of glass with "polished engraving". The engraver is named as "Kaulfurs" (Fr. J Kaulfuss is listed in the 1875–76 Edinburgh Directory with an address at 7 Queen's Place). In the same pattern book C70 is noted as a decanter, cut and engraved Rock Crystal. This speciality remained popular until well into the 20th century, although with the engraving much less detailed, and shallower.

In 1886 Edinburgh staged its most spectacular exhibition. Twenty-five acres of ground in West Meadows, between Melville Drive and Meadow Walk, housed the International Exhibition of Industry, Science and Art. The Meadows, or Hope Park, had been one of Edinburgh's lochs, the Borough Loch, but was drained during the early part of the 19th century. There were seven acres of buildings, a Grand Hall for exhibition purposes, and a "street" reproducing old Edinburgh buildings in which various crafts were demonstrated. The total cost was over £105,000, although the profit of £5500 gives one an idea of the success of the enterprise. There were four sections featuring glassware.

4   Glass of every description (Sheet, Plate, &c. Coloured).
5   Stained Glass for Architectural Purposes, &c.
6   Flint Glass or Crystal.
7   Bottle and Slag glass.

Jenkinson's "fine light-blown table glass" won a gold medal diploma. Other firms to achieve a similar distinction were Ford's Edinburgh, (Cut and engraved glass), Thomas Webb & Sons, Stourbridge, (Cut and other glass), and Stevens & Williams, Brierley Hill, (Art cameo glass). A reminder of this important exhibition is the arch of whales jawbones still standing at the southern end of Jawbone Walk.

Until 1914 Jenkinson continued to produce a wide range of high quality glass-ware. A large volume would be needed to describe in detail the variety of decorative, table and lighting glass-ware which left the works destined for customers in many parts of the British Isles and countries abroad. A summary of the more notable items in the pattern books is included at the end of the volume, but here could be mentioned some of the firm's customers and their orders. In 1879 Pitcairn's of New York was being supplied with table glass. In 1887 Parsons of Canada was a customer for sherbert (or sherbet) glasses, while the famous Tiffany's of New York during the early part of the 20th century received amongst other things a novelty "high ball tumbler". These are but a few names appearing in the firm's records, apart from those nearer home—in London, Birmingham, and Edinburgh (Ford's, for instance). Together with Government contracts

17. One of the firm's advertisements, late 1920s. (Edinburgh Crystal)

from such Departments as the Admiralty, these orders kept the firm extremely busy.

Alexander Dixson Jenkinson died on 27th March 1909. His success as a businessman is reflected in the value of his estate totalling almost £30,000. His place was taken by his son, Stanley Noel Jenkinson—the third and last generation of the family to have connections with the Edinburgh and Leith Flint Glass Works.

Stanley Noel Jenkinson was born in Edinburgh on 7th December 1886, his father residing at 4 Carlton Terrace. Educated at Edinburgh Academy, and Caius College, Cambridge, in 1913 he married Christabel Pottinger-Stephens. One of the 51 persons who assembled "to consider the formation of a Society of Glass Technology", he became very active in the affairs of the Society, in glass technology generally, and in refractories research. He served on the Joint Refractory Materials Committee, and on the Joint Conference of Scientific Societies on Refractories Research, making contributions on such subjects as the effects of sulphates on melting glass batches, on batch mixing and on pot-making. He was something of a pioneer in advocating the retailing of milk in glass bottles. In 1919 Stanley Jenkinson became President of the Society of Glass Technology, continuing to add to the industry's knowledge of clays and the drying of glass-house pots. In fact he was a pioneer in refractories research. Hitherto the suppliers of clays and users of pots blamed each other when things went wrong, but

NORTON PARK,
EDINBURGH.

IN THIS CATALOGUE will be found Illustrations of a very large variety of Fine Crystal Tableware, etc., for which these Works have long been noted.

WE have now the very latest and most up-to-date type of furnaces which it is possible to procure, and have taken advantage of all the facilities which modern science and research can give us, both in the selection of our chemicals, and the method of handling them.

THE result is that our Crystal is quite unsurpassable in its brilliance, lustre, and uniformity. Those interested have only to inspect our ware to verify the truth of our claims.

WE are fully alive to the great beauty of many of the early designs, and we would therefore specially draw your attention to our illustrations of " Period Reproductions."

THE Antique designs illustrated are reproductions of the best examples of old Glassware.

THESE reproductions should satisfy the requirements of all who devote considerable time and thought to their furnishing and desire to keep their table in harmony with their silver and furniture, but have hitherto been unable to do so, as only odd specimens of Antique glass are obtainable.

IN the event of our customers not finding what they require in this catalogue, we shall be pleased to submit designs for any articles which they may desire upon learning their precise requirements.

NOTE : It will be observed that the catalogue has extra guards at the end for attaching new sheets which we may issue from time to time.

EDINBURGH & LEITH FLINT GLASS WORKS.

1923.

18. Introduction to the 1923 catalogue. (Edinburgh Crystal)

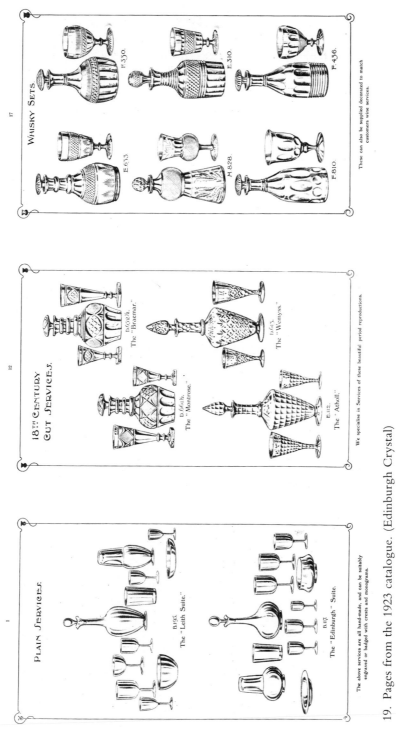

19. Pages from the 1923 catalogue. (Edinburgh Crystal)

neither did proper research to find the real reasons for pot failures. With the formation of Webb's Crystal Glass Company, referred to later, he managed the Company's Edinburgh and Stourbridge Works. He was director of BHF Syndicates Ltd., and Glass Engineering (Edinburgh) Co., Ltd., resigning in 1925. For some years Mr Jenkinson lived in Barcelona, dying there on 23rd June 1982, aged 95 years.

During the First World War the firm turned from producing mainly decorative and table glass to articles essential for the war effort—light bulbs, tubing, laboratory glass, and urgently needed apparatus. Naturally problems arose, including trouble over wages, and in 1915 Stanley Jenkinson visited Paris to recruit French workers, later importing craftsmen from Italy and Spain, one being Salvador Ysart, the first of the family to become famous in the history of Scottish glass. During 1915 Stanley Jenkinson refused orders from the Admiralty for hand-made goods in order to concentrate on other Government orders for essential ware.

A number of Jenkinson's workers had moved to the north of England and to Stourbridge and shortly after 1918, J Smith, the office manager went over to Stourbridge to try to win them back. Some did return and were instrumental in reviving certain pre-war specialities. Just as it had been most important for the firm to produce war goods, in the aftermath it was equally important for the firm to produce export articles to help restore the country's economy. Indeed the Edinburgh and Leith Flint Glass Works was one of the first British glass firms to return to normal peace time productions. After war-time austerity there was a world wide demand for fine quality glass. There were obvious difficulties in switching from war time productions, (most of which were no longer needed, and others which could not be produced economically under the new conditions) to peace time products, when most of the skilled craftsmen were not available.

Webb's Crystal Glass Co.

In 1921 the works at Norton Park was acquired by the newly formed Webb's Crystal Glass Company Ltd., and thus the connection with Thos. Webb & Sons of Dennis Glassworks, Stourbridge, became established on an official basis. Webb's Crystal Glass Company controlled not only the Stourbridge and Edinburgh glass firms, but also Duroglass, the London based firm at Queensborough, in addition to works at Tutbury. In 1931 they also acquired Henry G Richardson and Sons of Wordsley, near Stourbridge. The old established Richardson company, famous for over a century for its decorative and table glass, became mainly a wholesale business, with Duroglass producing principally lighting ware and electronic tubes.

The new company appointed Albert E Morris as General Manager at Edinburgh. Morris and Smith had worked together at Norton Park for 30 years, Morris in such capacities as Head Warehouseman and Glasshouse Foreman. Morris retired in 1924 to be replaced by R W Edmunds with John Mitchell as Office Manager.

The company immediately set about modernising the Norton Park works and establishing the firm's normal productions. The re-organisation, carried out during a time of rising prices, was costly. Fortunately, the effort paid off, the demand for Edinburgh Crystal glass continuously increasing during the 1920s.

One notable development at the works was the installation in 1921 of a patent recuperative furnace—the first of its kind in the country. The old type furnace was uneconomic and inefficient. The new type not only produced glass of better quality but consumed approximately one-third the amount of coal used by the old—a great saving in fuel and labour costs. Pyrometers and recorders, by which furnace temperatures could be read every minute of the day or night, ensured a control essential to reliable quality production of glass. By 1927 a second recuperative furnace was in use. During this period more scientific methods were introduced in dealing with the various ingredients used in glass-making. The previous "rule-of-thumb" ways were abandoned, thus obviating variations in quality.

During the 1920s the first stage in cut decoration on glass was achieved by means of mild steel wheels. The cutter held the glass against a revolving wheel fed from above by a stream of sand and water. The rough cuts were then smoothed by another craftsman using a wheel made of the finest type of stone for the purpose—a local stone from Edinburgh's Craigleith quarries. Even then the surface of the decorated parts was matt and appeared dull. To restore the former surface brilliance the cut decoration then had to be polished. Formerly this was done by using wood and cork wheels, and brushes impregnated with putty powder (mainly red lead and tin oxide), a lengthy and most unhealthy, even lethal, process. A quicker and much more economical way was introduced in the 1920s, by dipping the cut glasses into a mixture of hydrofluoric and sulphuric acids. "Acid polishing" restored the brilliance of the surface of the cut patterns in seconds rather than minutes: with the old method polishing often took longer than the actual cutting.

A Pottery Gazette notice of the firm's products during the period mentions, apart from individual pieces, "countless handsome designs in glass-ware both for strictly utilitarian and ornamental purposes".

Mainly responsible for the modernisation of the cutting department was foreman Harry Moyle, doing an excellent job for nearly 30 years, training many first-class cutters who were able to keep up the tradition after he retired in 1948. Moyle's well earned retirement unfortunately lasted for only two years. He died in 1950.

The decade saw the battle against the dumping of foreign glass begin in earnest. Large quantities were being imported into the British Isles, yet, in

D

20. Group of Edinburgh Crystal marked pieces of the 1930s—including two 8″ vases and one
6″ vase (L736), one oval violet bowl (K258) and honey jar. (Author's collection)

1926 the Board of Trade unhelpfully decreed that the British glass industry
was not eligible for protection. Thus the home industry had to rely entirely
on its own efforts to combat the serious foreign competition. To command a
necessary share of the home and world markets, Edinburgh and Leith Flint
Glass Works relied mainly on quality and, to some extent, on innovation.

In 1923 the retailers Robert Hogg and Co. of Belfast, put on a show of
cut glass, with demonstrations of cutting by Norton Park craftsmen.

As proof of the firm's progress, at the 1925–26 Dunedin Exhibition the
Norton Park firm achieved the great distinction of being awarded the First
and Special Order of Merit, and Gold Medal for their high quality glass.

One innovation of the period was a patent, taken out on the 3rd May
1926, for "an improved loud speaker for wireless sets". This was the
attractive Edina Table Lamp, pattern numbers K237 and 238, with a loud
speaker unit in its base, mentioned in the following.

During January 1927 a member of "The Weekly Scotsman" staff visited
the Norton Park Works, and an account of his tour of the factory appears in
that journal. He was taken round the mixing house where the "batch"
(ingredients used in making glass) was being prepared. Firstly the silver sand
from Fontainebleau in France, then the other ingredients all carefully dried,
refined, weighed and mixed in definite proportions, a mechanical sieve with

a 40 mesh screen, being used in the process. The writer mentions the improved recuperative type furnaces, and the glassmakers—"so many magicians creating beautiful things out of a clear liquid." After admiring the various stages of glass decoration, particularly cutting and engraving, the reporter concludes his description: "As I prepared to leave, orchestral music poured forth from a hidden source. Such purity of tone surely did not come from a loud speaker. No loud speaker was to be seen, nevertheless it was there. My guide pointed to a handsome crystal lamp on the table. The cutting concealed the magnetic unit in the base. The sound deflector was fashioned by the lamp shade. A novelty, but unlike so many novelties, one which is surely of practical use."

Another novelty, patented on 11th February 1930, was "a glass flower holder or vase for use primarily in motor vehicles or yachts", copyright of the design, subsisting for five years, being granted to "Webb's Crystal Glass Company Limited, sole proprietors of The Edinburgh and Leith Flint Glass Works".

The following year the firm was advertising something more than luxury items—productions in collaboration with Duro-Ray. These were Duro-Ray silvered reflectors, floodlights and pendant lights, made by the "Barnes Patent Silvering Process", a process used by the British Navy exclusively for search-light mirrors since 1916. The floodlights were weather-proof and proof against sea water, producing a concentrated beam of up to 1550 candle-power using a 200 watt lamp. The glass consisted of Edinburgh optical crystal glass "the purest obtainable absorbing less light than any other known glass" and "the thick film of silver backed by layers of pure copper and lead, electrolytically applied, and forming one single indivisible whole, so closely attached to the glass as to prevent completely the percolation of air or moisture. The Reflector is, therefore, untarnishable, even if immersed in sea water". A larger model used a 500 watt lamp. A smaller more mobile standard model used a 200 watt lamp.

The pendant lights were mainly for display purposes. Edinburgh optical glass was again used, but superimposed upon it was a thin film of coloured glass—five natural colours: golden amber, green, amethyst, ruby, and daylight blue. The light of the lamp (100, 150, or 200 watts) had to pass through the coloured glass to the silver film, and back again, before the light reached the object to be illuminated. The reflected light picked up the colour in the most natural way possible and flooded the object "with the sympathetic tint drawn from the glass. The effect upon objects of kindred colour illuminated by the Duro-Ray method was to throw them into relief and display them in their true daylight hues, enriched, but without exaggeration."

In spite of the economic situation at home, and the competition against foreign glass imports, the firm did develop steadily during the 1930s, but

THE "THISTLE" SERVICE
H.828
CUT & ENGRAVED.

FINGER BOWL.

WHISKY TOT SMALL SIZE. WHISKY TOT LARGE SIZE. ½ PT. TUMBLER. QUART JUG.

GOBLET. CHAMPAGNE. CLARET. QUART DECANTER. LIQUEUR. COCKTAIL. PORT. SHERRY.

21. Advertisement for "Thistle" service. (Edinburgh Crystal)

only with great difficulty. Mr George Gay covers the trying period in his contribution to this history of the company.

In an effort to further publicise Edinburgh's products, the firm exhibited at the 1932 Scottish Ideal Home Exhibition, where a Norton Park glass-cutter again demonstrated his skills.

A healthy trade was being carried on with the British Dominions and America. Deep cut patterns came into fashion again, with the Thistle design popular amongst the Scots and Americans. In August 1933 the Edinburgh "Evening News" mentions two further popular items: crystal glass with "mirror" patterns cut into the design, and the newest "craze", a white crystal glass shading into amber. At that time the reporter reveals that Edinburgh was producing crystal, ruby, green, blue, and amber, a statement confirmed by reference to the firm's "P" pattern book, which also illustrates two other colours, mauve and citron.

In 1938 Arnold Fleming, author of "Scottish and Jacobite Glass" made highly complimentary remarks about Edinburgh and Leith Flint Glass Company products. "The dazzling quality of Norton Park glass, whether decorative or useful, rivals that made in the halcyon days of the trade, and so reproductions of antique style are a specialty of this company. Here we have candlesticks, candelabra and S-shaped girandoles alongside the latest patterns of electric lamps. The limpid nature of glass is charmingly displayed in cut goblets, vases and flower bowls of most chaste designs, a bewildering display glittering and sparkling in a thousand lights . . . This company has had lately the honour of supplying Holyrood Palace with an exquisite set of cut glass for the Royal Banquets."

In 1939, on the eve of the outbreak of the Second World War, the company had a workforce of 260. The war again caused the firm to cease their normal products and concentrate on glass needed for the war effort, mainly components for newly invented radar equipment, especially large numbers of glass envelopes for cathode ray tubes.

After the Second World War the firm had again to re-stablish itself as a producer of fine quality crystal glass for the table and for decoration. There was no lack of orders from both home and overseas markets. Skilled and experienced craftsmen were no longer available and a new generation lacking both skills and experience appeared, with a different outlook. National Service added to the firm's difficulties.

In 1948, replacing Harry Moyle, Stewart Somerville took charge of the cutting shop, and remained until 1954 when he moved to a similar position with the Montreal firm, The Phillips Cut Glass Company, who specialised in decorating blanks imported from Europe.

During 1951 Kenneth Northwood succeeded H F Baraclough as Works Manager. Mr Northwood took over at a time when a very difficult labour situation needed handling with great tact and diplomacy. Mr Northwood, son of John Northwood II, of Stourbridge glass fame, writes an interesting account, included in this volume, of his 25 years with the Edinburgh glass firm.

During February 1951 an informative article appeared in "The Weekly Scotsman" describing and illustrating the Norton Park Works. Reproductions of photographs show a selection of glassware made at Norton Park, Tommy Melville "warming in" a jug, Fred Lonie engraving part of a Thistle design glass, blanks being cut by carborundum wheels, Vincel Maxa (a Czech) blowing a salad bowl, Tom White showing John Smith how to put a cross button stem on a sherbert glass for a Canadian order, and Dessie Burgoyne operating the process known as "cracking off"—a semi-automatic operation to remove surplus glass after blowing and annealing.

Another innovation in 1952 was the pressed glass production formerly undertaken by John Walsh Walsh, the long established Birmingham firm, which closed down that year. Pressed products included bowls, dishes, jugs and lenses.

When Stewart Somerville left the firm for Canada in 1954, George R Gay succeeded him, taking charge of the cutting shop. "The Pottery Gazette" of December 1954 describes Mr Gay as "a typical hard-working

22. Thistle service H828. (Courtesy, Huntly House Museum)

Scotsman who has made a particular study of the history of Scottish glass ware and the factories who have been thus engaged. He is well regarded by both management and the men". Fortunately, Mr Gay has been able to describe his service at Norton Park later in this work.

At this time General Manager was John Mitchell who had served in that important post since 1930. In 1954 there were 14 "chairs" (teams of glassmakers making a variety of articles) operating a two shift system. Altogether there were 200 employees working on the one acre Norton Park site. The firm produced a wide range of stemware, bowls, and vases. In the factory were three modern ten-pot furnaces, plus a two-pot oil fired furnace for making soda lime glass in red, amber, and green colours for traffic light and other coloured lenses. Glass was annealed in two Amco lehrs heated by town's gas. A flourishing trade with Commonwealth countries, and the USA, continued.

In 1955, the old name of Edinburgh and Leith Flint Glass Works, or Company, in use for almost eighty years, was changed to "The Edinburgh Crystal Glass Co." This was not only simpler, but appropriate, because for half a century the firm had been the only one in Edinburgh producing crystal glass.

During October 1958 the rather unimaginative showroom was replaced. New mahogany display units were installed and a more modern colour scheme introduced sky blue, deep red and pastel grey. In 1961 the showrooms were described as being like a "glittering ice palace", with the glass as "beautiful, perfectly made, and mostly entirely functional". There was no attempt to be "outrageously futuristic" but the firm was modern enough to meet contemporary needs, including demands for octagonal shaped salad bowls, hors d'oeuvres sets, and contemporary glasses for gin and tonic. At that time Mr M B Tulloch was General Manager.

Whisky

Whisky is often regarded as Scotland's national beverage. At one time the art of distilling was part of a Highlander's education, but now the craft is carried on commercially by distilleries in various parts of the mainland and islands. Whisky gets its name from the Gaelic "uisge beatha" meaning "water of life". Fine single malt or grain whiskies are produced and sold in their original state when mature, or blended together and retailed under proprietory names. Scotch whisky gets its unique flavour and quality particularly from Scottish air, soft water from streams flowing through granite, and from the peat used in distilling. It seems appropriate that decanters and drinking glasses made from fine Scottish crystal glass should be used when "Scotch" is consumed!

One Norton Park production was a whisky decanter for the well known Ballantine firm. More than 35,000 of these were exported during the late 1950s, each cut with a traditional hobnail diamond pattern on the lower part; the upper part left plain for the label. Filled with venerable whisky they found a welcome in many homes throughout the world. The firm had the added benefit of receiving orders for additional services to complement the decanters.

During the decade following the Second World War Edinburgh Crystal became highly regarded in the Western Hemisphere. The Cunard Company's "Ocean Times" in July 1960 quotes the case of a New York antique dealer, who, on being asked by a collector where he could get replacements of some fine crystal balls missing from a Fabergé silver epergne, advised him to approach the Norton Park firm.

Schmidt and Sons of Los Angeles and San Francisco, Tiffany's and Gimbels of New York, and Eatons and Hudson Bay Company of Canada,

23. Cameo fleur tumbler vase. M451 *c*. 1931 H 7½″. (Author's collection)

had been distributing Edinburgh Crystal glass for years, some buying large quantities for their customers' special requirements.

Around 1960 approximately 40% of the firm's products was destined for overseas markets, including not only major countries such as America and Canada, but ones such as the Fiji Islands and Ghana. The Government of the latter placed a large order for glassware decorated with a new pattern, the "Ghana Star", an adaptation of the "Edinburgh Star".

During the early 1960s it was evident that the works at Norton Park was becoming inadequate. Hemmed in by the railway, and other factories, modernisation and expansion were impossible. In 1964 the prospects of building a new modern works became more of a reality. In that year Webb's Crystal Glass Company Limited (Thos. Webb and Sons and Edinburgh Crystal) was acquired by Crown House Limited. In 1971 the Company was merged with Dema Glass, based at Chesterfield, another Crown House subsidiary.

Mr George Gay writes:
"I started work as an apprentice glass cutter with the Edinburgh and Leith Flint Glass Works, as it was then called, in 1928. The factory was situated at Norton Park, Abbeyhill, on the eastern side of Edinburgh, and no great distance from Holyrood Palace. In 1928, the factory was very busy, overtime being worked in both the glasshouse and the decorating departments, along with the various auxiliary departments. At that time, just before the severe slump in the early 1930s, the cutting or decorating department comprised four distinct cutting shops, as well as an engraving and intaglio section. Altogether, there was almost one hundred employees in this department.

The cutters were divided into 'roughers' and 'smoothers', there being approximately three times as many smoothers as roughers. During that period day-work on a fixed wage was the basic method of payment, with roughers averaging £3 5s. a week, and smoothers £3.

Each cutting shop had about 25 cutting frames with steel wheels using fine white sand and carborundum for roughing, and stone wheels for smoothing, each frame being driven by a flat belt attached to a spindle, the 25 spindles being attached to a central shaft. The rougher had to be something of an engineer. To maintain the required shape of a steel wheel it was necessary from time to time to remove the spindle from the frame and after fixing it to an engineer's lathe the edge of the wheel was turned and so re-shaped.

The lubricant for roughing was a mixture of fine white sand and water which ran freely down a runner on to the wheel. For roughing it was traditional for the wheel to run towards the operator, while for smoothing, the wheel revolved away from the operator. For smoothing, water was the lubricant, the smoother going over each roughed out cut.

24. Goblet engraved with view of Edinburgh Castle from the Grassmarket, possibly made at
    Norton Park, c. 1890. (Private collection)

On the whole, patterns tended to be fairly elaborate with the decorating covering most of the surface. Salad bowls, sugars and creams, vases, jelly dishes, butter plates, jugs, decanters along with wine services and tumblers were the most common objects decorated. The glasshouse had many capable blowers and excellent hand made 'chairs' who turned out perfect reproductions of eighteenth and nineteenth century glass. Quite a number of these reproductions were of fine light glasses, but many, such as candlesticks etc., were extensively decorated.

When I commenced my apprenticeship all the traditional types of cutting were undertaken at Norton Park. For example, scalloping was a regular feature of many of the patterns. Relatively few simple patterns were turned out, most open diamond patterns being either laced or checkered. Raised diamonds were a common feature as were steps of rings on wine services, vases etc. Variations of the Thistle pattern, with its raised diamonds, cut leg, star foot, short flutes and thistle engraving (usually near the top rim of the particular glass) were extensively produced.

In the early 1930s, as the general economic situation deteriorated and blowers and cutters were put on short time, or in some cases, became unemployed, the type of articles produced, and patterns executed, tended to change. Less elaborate cutting, and so less expensive ware, became the norm. Piecework was introduced to increase production, and make the factory more competitive. In the middle 1930s carborundum powder took the place of sand for roughing as it proved a better abrasive, allowing work to be produced more quickly. Carborundum powder also allowed roughing to be done with fewer chipped edges, particularly for mitre work, and so allowed for deeper cutting which produced greater brilliance or reflection when polished.

During the War years, and especially when Lease Lend became effective from 1940 onwards, very little cut ware was produced. Most of the cutters who were eligible in terms of age, served in the forces, and those who remained were employed mainly in work concerned with the production of technical glass needed for war purposes.

With the end of the war, and the return of servicemen to civilian life, the factory returned to the production of high quality decorative ware. Very soon after the resumption of work in the decorating department, carborundum wheels began to be used instead of steel wheels, for roughing purposes. The great advantage of carborundum wheels was that they could be turned or re-shaped in the frame without requiring turning in a special lathe. Another advantage was the time saved in no longer being required to clean or wash the carborundum powder. The final advantage was that, provided the carborundum wheel was kept 'open', it was a better abrasive than the steel wheel with carborundum powder.

About this time too, experiments began to take place using diamond

25. Wine glass cooler, engraved with hunting scene. (Edinburgh Crystal)

impregnated wheels. In the early days they were used for relatively light but deeply cut patterns, allowing cutters to complete the decoration in one operation for the majority of articles. Since then, their use has become much more extensive, and has allowed some speed up in production, but they are of course much more expensive than carborundum wheels, or either quarried, or synthetic stones.

Perhaps the biggest change in the last 30 years or so, has been the proportion of tumblers and stemware produced and decorated as compared to the pre-war period. Patterns are of course, by and large, less elaborate, but the quantities produced are now enormous. Individual cutting lathes with special attachments to make the operator's life easier are now the order of the day. Perhaps it is a sign of growing old, but for all the disadvantages associated with the older methods and techniques, I cannot help feeling that the final product took a lot of beating."

Mr Kenneth Northwood writes:

"It was late in 1950 that I first visited Edinburgh and Leith Flint Glass Works situated on the restricted Norton Park site where it had been producing glassware since the turn of the century. I was happy to take the vacant position of Works Manager early in 1951 with a particular mandate to develop the technical aspects of the factory.

The works was then recovering from the effects of the war, both in equipment and personnel. In the glasshouse it was particularly apparent that the average age of the employees was too high for future prospects. It was not possible to obtain the services of trained glassmakers from outside sources—the powerful Union would not agree to this solution anyway—therefore the recruitment and training of young men was immediately instituted.

With the co-operation of the Union a training scheme with an instructor was set up so that when the Government's national training plan for industry became law in the 1960s the factory was able to implement its rules with a minimum of difficulty. However, a problem occurred in training enough glass cutters as the Union insisted on a ratio of five journeymen to one apprentice, which obviously did not give any margin for increase in skilled men. This restriction was not altered for several years, consequently any increase in cut glass output had to be derived from increased productivity. In 1951 a new ten-pot recuperative glass melting furnace was completed to replace old equipment which had come to the end of its useful life. This furnace continued to produce crystal glass until the Norton Park site was closed and the factory demolished in 1974. During the 1957–60 period, advantage was taken of the availability of cheap supplies of fuel oil to change all the glass melting equipment, which was burning local coal, using instead the 'black liquid'. This move, more than any other which took place during my time at Norton Park, improved working conditions in the old factory. The soot and sulphur content of the atmosphere decreased considerably and enabled us to give the buildings a 'wash and brush-up', with beneficial results to working conditions and recruitment. Glass cutting was carried out in one large shop situated on the first floor over the warehouse together with small outbuildings. In order to bring the cutting staff into one department a new building was erected circa 1960, which eliminated the scattered old buildings, gave a better engraving department and increased warehouse storage space. A new showroom with modern display and lighting was opened in 1957.

The parent Company—Webbs Crystal Glass Company—was bought by Crown House in 1964 and thus Edinburgh Crystal, as it by then had become known, later formed part of the Dema Glass section of that Group. With the resources of the new owners it became possible to build an entirely new works on an open site outside the city boundary. Plans were drawn for a factory to be built on modern lines and the move was made in two stages—the 'cold end' consisting of decorating, polishing, warehousing, engineering and sales moved in 1969. The 'hot end' where the glass was actually melted and shaped into articles remained for a while at Norton Park. The final transfer of the furnaces, mixing department, pot making, processing and the remainder of the engineering section to the newly completed factory at Penicuik was made in 1974. The old site near Easter Road was sold shortly afterwards and the buildings were completely demolished.

When I first went to Edinburgh I was a little apprehensive—an Englishman amongst so many Scots—but I soon found reassurance as everyone co-operated to try to make the only existing Scottish Crystal Glass factory a successful one. Annual works outings and children's Christmas parties were occasions of happy memories which did a great deal to bring everyone together. It is not possible to mention all the many Edinburgh workers who gave such good service during my 25 years but there are a few I can remember with gratitude for the help so willingly given over the years. John Mitchell, General Manager for some years, was well-known in all the Scottish cities where he regularly sold the products of the factory. Harry Coxon; John Morris; David Mackenzie and Jack Blaik were Departmental Managers who are now deceased but who will always be remembered with affection and thanks.

Many employees are carrying on the Edinburgh tradition in the Penicuik factory and to them I wish 'good luck' and many years of prosperity."

The move to a new site is described in a later chapter.

26. Reproductions of Jacobite glasses, 1920s. (Edinburgh Crystal)

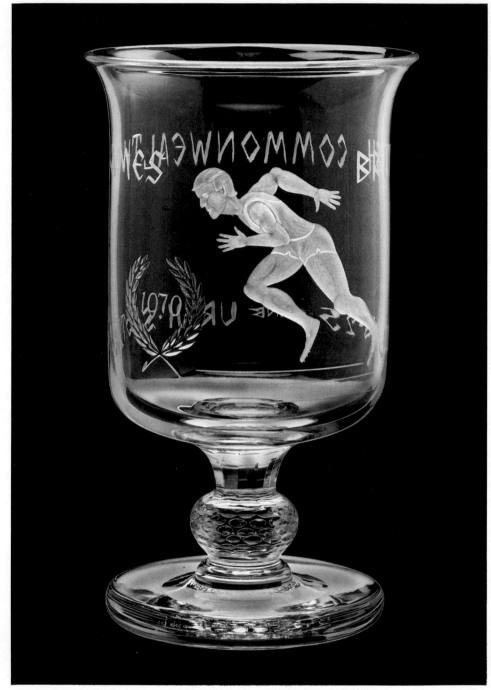

27. Commonwealth Games, Edinburgh, 1970. H 9″. (Edinburgh Crystal)

28. View of Penicuik works. (Edinburgh Crystal)

4. Penicuik

The highly significant period in the history of Edinburgh Crystal is dealt with by Mr Northwood and Mr Dempster in their contributions. The decision to move out of the city, made with some regret, was forced upon the Company through lack of a suitable site within the city boundaries and the advantage of improved grants if a new works was built in a development area. A 7½ acre site on the Eastfield Industrial Estate, Penicuik, ten miles south of Norton Park, was purchased.

Penicuik lies amongst the foothills of the Pentland Hills, Stevenson's "hills of home", deriving their name from the ancient settlers' "Pict land". The name Penicuik is also of ancient origin, from the Gaelic "pen-y-cog"— the hill of the cuckoo. In its long history the town has had a mixed agricultural and industrial economy: sheep and cattle rearing, with paper making and iron founding. The nucleus of the old town was on the River Esk, but in recent years there has been something of an urban spread. The countryside around is still attractive, with the Pentlands themselves dominating the western skyline and the Moorfoots the eastern.

The two stage development began with an 11,000 sq. ft. cutting shop with the ancillaries, engraving, polishing, packaging and despatch. This was officially opened on 1st August 1969 by Mr William Ross, Secretary of State for Scotland. After a brief ceremony lasting only a few minutes, Mr Ross then toured the works for approximately 45 minutes, saying how extremely impressed he had been by the high standard of workmanship and the general layout of the factory. To mark the event Mr and Mrs Ross were presented with glass ware. As Mr Dempster mentions in his contribution, there were obvious difficulties in operating glass making and glass decorating ten miles apart, and teething troubles followed when the glass making side did eventually move from Norton Park to Penicuik in 1974. Mr Dempster also describes the various developments and improvements at the Penicuik works during the past ten years. In 1969 the firm had 250 employees, more than half working at Penicuik. Like many other manufacturing firms, Edinburgh Crystal had a challenge and problems in a wider field.

In 1973 Britain became a full member of the European Economic Community, the Common Market, and the firm entered a strong, competitive and sophisticated market. It was anticipated that the new works would produce 750,000 pieces a year. This figure is currently being exceeded.

29. Goblets. Forth and Severn Bridges openings, 1964 and 1966. H 6¾". (Edinburgh Crystal)

Present day visitors will be pleased with the efficient way in which guided tours of the works are conducted, enabling the skills of both the glassmakers and decorators to be better appreciated and admired. They will also enjoy the excellent facilities, and above all, be impressed by the quality of Edinburgh Crystal glass.

Mr Gilbert Dempster writes:
"Accustomed as I was with an engineering background to what Blake described as 'dark Satanic mills' I was still appalled at the sight of Norton Park in 1969. How was it possible for such a beautiful product to come out of these dreadful conditions? Norton Park had been occupied since 1876 in this work and it was a tribute to the skill and endurance of the employees that there had been almost a century of building a worldwide reputation for artistic and exquisite crystal glass manufacture.

— 57 —

Of course, it was inefficient, losses were high and morale low. Conditions led to distrust and security was non-existent. Even the method of wage calculation had been devised in the distant past and had now lost its meaning and effect. Though they had been associate companies since 1921, Thomas Webb at Stourbridge and Edinburgh Crystal were far more than 300 miles apart, for the staff at one had little knowledge of their counterparts at the other. A lifetime of experience in making the same composition of glass was never shared or compared.

It was the infusion of substantial financial support by the new owners, Crown House, which made possible the radical changes that were enacted over the next decade, changes not just of a physical or technical nature but also of attitudes and relationships among employees. When the very specialised nature of crystal glass manufacture and the power of inevitable resistance to change in a labour intensive industry are taken into account, a decade is not a long time.

The opening in 1969 of a new factory at Penicuik, 10 miles from Norton Park, enabled the transfer there of the Cold End Processes, comprising marking of blank or plain glass, cutting and engraving of patterns on the glass, acid polishing and final inspection with grading, wrapping and packaging. A spacious warehouse with despatch facilities and new administrative offices and showroom were included. Some shuffling around of operations at Norton Park was possible but the factory was still cramped for the remaining processes.

Change was in the air and a new future was there to be formed, fought for and won. It was not clearly seen by all, however, so there were fears and suspicions as well as hopes and dreams. From a management view, it received considerable impetus from the difficulties experienced in trying to operate efficiently with a manufacturing cycle divided down the middle by road 10 miles long. A new and meaningful wage system was introduced and a limited amount of experimentation on glass melting and forming using butane gas instead of oil was undertaken. The battle was on and with widening involvement of personnel, morale was improving. This was illustrated when, because of national power cuts, glassmaking at one stage was only possible in *12* hour shifts three times per week. The glassmakers wielded hot irons for the full shift even though their seasoned hands were painfully raw. Experiences in adversity frequently draw people together and I can understand those who today from a position of relative comfort and safety refer to 'the good old days at Norton Park'.

The process of moving the Hot End to Penicuik was long and slow, or so it felt at the time, but that was to prove well worthwhile. Management, Union and Workpeople were formed into consultative groups to come up with the best ideas from managerial and practical experience. These groups contributed to the planning of the new factory in both building and equipment terms, to the method of training personnel in the skills required, to the organisation of the actual move stage by stage and to the operation of production in an entirely different environment. During the course of construction of the new glasshouse, personnel visited the site from Norton Park. During the period consultations commenced with Stourbridge personnel, with interchange of experience and work which happily have continued ever since. The move was accomplished without serious hitch or delay and a few weeks later, in 1974, Norton Park was finally demolished.

Despite all the care in preparation, serious problems were encountered in the new glasshouse. The ventilation system did not work properly and its revision took months to complete. Twelve single-pot furnaces fired by butane had been built and six lehrs had been installed, the emphasis being on the flexibility offered by such an individual range of equipment. It had been anticipated that the glass melting period could be reduced to overnight but after testing many methods it had to be admitted that this could not be achieved satisfactorily in all types of work with the full lead crystal which was our hallmark. Production arrangements had to be adjusted and a two-pot furnace introduced to provide additional capacity. The period of dealing with these difficulties was alarmingly long and the pressures on all employees correspondingly high. I believe it was the degree of participation that had produced a deeper understanding and appreciation of the problems to the employees who in the midst of frustration displayed considerable patience and co-operation.

Of many new features, the principal differences were a sophisticated mixing plant, humidity controlled accommodation for the making of pots and refractories, a forklift truck with which the arduous and often dangerous job of changing pots was transformed with fewer men in a quarter of the time in more safety and less discomfort, and the reduction of a pair of wine glass making teams from eight to seven persons. This last point meant that boys training to be glassmakers would take part in production earlier and not be disheartened at an initial stage with continual unskilled work.

As the site at Penicuik began to operate as a complete unit, further developments were justified and embarked upon with success. Natural gas became available and was introduced without difficulty while retaining butane firing as an alternative. Limited production of second quality only has been undertaken by an automatic cutting machine. More sophisticated equipment has been installed for grinding and finishing edges and rims and for cracking off the tops of blown glass. Since the cutting shop was built in 1969 there has been steady and careful development of high speed diamond impregnated wheel cutting. A further two-pot furnace has been built and another acid polishing plant established. An entirely new department has been built to house the sand-etching process which has achieved great accuracy in reproducing artwork on glass and complements the traditional and more expensive engraving. Some dimensional effect can also be obtained and this process has grown rapidly with further potential.

A notable feature in recent years has been the growth of industry's direct approach to the public. Whilst visits through the factory at Norton Park and at Penicuik have always been arranged, the interest aroused was such that an extension of this facility for tourists was highly desirable. A modern office block adjacent to the factory in Penicuik was purchased and converted in 1982 to provide a spacious shop and reception area for visitors. Guided tours of the factory take place each working day and there is also a fine cafeteria, all for the fascination and comfort of visitors.

When Edinburgh Crystal first went to Penicuik in 1969 it was described as a papermaking town. The paper mills unhappily have all closed down and crystal glassmaking is now the main industry, extending in 1982 to 350 employees. The very nature of that industry depends on the skills of its employees and an intensive training policy is essential. Many young persons have been brought in locally now and have shown great adaptability to the skills of long ago. Moreover, they too have been filled with the same pride and enthusiasm for the production of Edinburgh Crystal as those before them and they will obviously carry on that tradition with care and with honour."

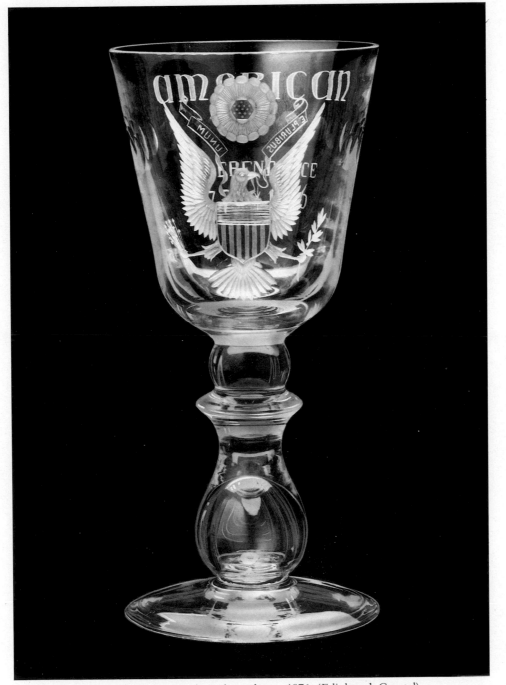

30. Goblet. Bicentenary of American Independence, 1976. (Edinburgh Crystal)

31. Decanter and goblet. Queen Mother's 80th birthday, 1980. (Decanter, H 11¾″) (Edinburgh Crystal)

32. Square decanter. Royal Wedding, 1981. H 12″. (Edinburgh Crystal)

33. The Master's Miniatures, 1978. (Edinburgh Crystal)

5. The Manufacture of Glass

Edinburgh Crystal glass owes its fine quality to a number of factors: the ingredients, the equipment, the careful control of all stages of manufacture, and the skills of designers, technicians, and craftsmen. But all these factors have to result in a successful commercial venture, and here a management team, backed by marketing and sales personnel, ensures that this is so.

Ingredients

The raw materials which form the "batch" must be of the purest possible quality, with chemical and physical consistency, and be carefully prepared and accurately blended. The main constituent is silica (silicon dioxide) in the form of sand, which comes mainly from Loch Aline, a narrow sea loch on the west coast of Scotland, opening into the Sound of Mull. The deposit is quite unique, the sand being obtained by highly sophisticated mining techniques at the underground operation. This silver white sand has an extremely low iron oxide content, averaging only 0.01%, and is carefully graded for particle size. The high quality of the silica is necessary for producing finest quality crystal glass, avoiding any distinct and undesirable yellow/green colourisation due to the presence of iron oxide. The second most important constituent in Edinburgh Crystal glass is highly refined lead (lead oxide). This ingredient imparts unique properties to crystal glass, making it softer and less brittle, enabling the glass to be more readily cut and polished. It makes the glass more dense and gives it weight. Lead crystal glasses have a distinctive "ring" when lightly tapped. The presence of lead oxide also increases the refractive index, creating a brilliance, especially when cut, akin to that of the finest natural rock crystal, which the glass maker through the centuries has sought to emulate.

Potash in the form of potassium carbonate or bicarbonate, and potassium nitrate introduce alkali into the glass, acting as fluxing and oxidising agents, and improving the clarity of the glass. Other minor ingredients also act as fluxing, refining and oxidising agents, thereby aiding the melting process and enhancing the physical properties of the glass for the glassmaker, making it softer and more pliable for his use. Nickel and cobalt oxides act as decolourisers, ensuring that any tinge of yellow or green is masked by an indiscernible, more desirable blue/purple tint.

The proportions of the main constituent oxides forming Edinburgh Crystal glass are 50% silica, 36% lead and 12% potassium. It is interesting to note that the silica, lead oxide and potassium oxide content of British crystal glass has varied little since the time, 300 years ago, when George Ravenscroft and Hawley Bishopp perfected lead crystal glass, Britain's greatest contribution to the world of glass.

The ingredients having been accurately weighed, they must be mixed so that the batch forms a homogeneous whole. To the raw materials is added "cullet": Edinburgh Crystal "waste" glass accumulated at various stges of manufacturing processes. This re-cycling of "waste" glass, approximately one-third in proportion of the whole "batch", assists in the melting process.

Glass melting is carried out in clay crucibles known as "pots".

Pots

In the old days clay arrived in dry powder form and had to be wetted and trampled, but now clay for pot making arrives ready for use—homogeneous with air expelled. Yet, as a precaution and by tradition, the Edinburgh Crystal potmaker puts his clay through a pugmill: the clay mix is basically a natural siliceous clay mined near Halifax, Yorkshire, which provides resistance to thermal shock created by temperature fluctuations during melting processes. Aluminous clay is added to provide chemical durability, combating the corrosive effects of molten glass. Mixed with these natural clays is "grog"—siliceous clay fired and pulverised, representing approximately one quarter of the whole. The low iron content of the clay, as with batch materials, is most important.

Potmaking techniques have scarcely changed during the past century. The clay is made up into convenient sausage shape lumps of "plasticine" consistency. The clay for the bottom of the pot is spread on a special board which has handles, to a thickness of approximately four inches, within a metal ring to regulate pot diameter. The board is then reversed, transferring the pot bottom to another board, on which is spread powdered "grog".

The pot is slowly built up in circular fashion by deft manipulation of the clay lumps, the potmaker using his hand and fingers to construct the pot and to prevent the enclosure of air. Sometimes a mould, a wooden plug, is used in the process, but most pots are shaped completely by hand. During this process short controlled drying out periods are essential for the pots to harden. In the final stage the dome is constructed, also shaped completely by hand. When the dome is finished a small hole is left, air is blown in, the hole sealed, the air preventing any slight collapse of the dome.

Next day a hole is cut to let the air out and soon afterwards this is converted into a larger hole which forms the mouth through which blow-irons will be inserted. At all stages the potmaker must ensure that there are no air pockets in the clay to render the pot structure weak.

34. "Breath of Scotland" series, with early use of sand etching, 1978. (Edinburgh Crystal)

Normally nine pots are made over a period of four weeks in a special room where temperature and humidity can be strictly controlled.

Afterwards the pots are stored in dry warm conditions for about five months. The interior is then vacuum cleaned and the pot, an "igloo" shape crucible in a "green" state, is ready for the "pot arch". In this special kiln a controlled temperature rise up to 1200°C, lasting five days, prepares the pot for the start of its working life. Due to the gradual corrosive effect of molten glass on the pot the average life in the furnace is only eight weeks.

The pot replacing process known as "pot setting" has to be carried out in great heat, as it is not practicable to reduce the temperature in the furnace. The front wall of the furnace is broken down and the old pot removed. To minimise heat loss and risk of fracture, the new pot is then transferred to the furnace as speedily as possible. The wall is then rebuilt, leaving the pot mouth exposed. In this spectacular operation lasting fifteen minutes and involving a team of five men, a fork-lift truck has replaced the old manually operated carriage.

Two essential auxiliaries to the pots are the rings and stoppers. These are made within the works, using raw clay from Bonnybridge and Dykehead. The rings are made in two half circles which float on the surface of the molten glass inside the pot and "weld" together. The inner circle provides a small working area from which any impurities can easily be skimmed.

A stopper is placed in the mouth of each pot during the melting process to prevent heat loss when the pot is not being worked, and is subsequently removed when this process is completed and the molten glass is ready for cooling to working temperature. Each pot rests on fire bricks and form blocks are built up in front of the pot almost as far as the lip of the pot mouth, the enclosing being completed with fire bricks. The form blocks and bricks are plastered with clay which soon dries with the heat from the furnace. Thus the pot is sealed into the furnace. Three holes are left in the new brickwork—one exposing the mouth of the pot, through which the blow-iron can be inserted to gather the molten glass for making the glass article. The other two apertures, known as "shoes" allow for re-heating the nozzle ends of the blow irons.

Each pot will hold approximately 800kg of glass. The melting cycle lasts for 24 hours, with a furnace temperature of 1400°C. The furnace is then cooled to a working temperature for the glass, of between 1080° and 1150°, depending upon the type of article to be produced. For example, smaller pieces need the higher temperature to lower the viscosity of the glass.

Glassmaking

The basic processes and tools used in the production of hand-made glass have changed little in the last 2000 years. Around 50BC glassmakers in the Middle East discovered that a hollow vessel could be produced by gathering glass in a viscous state on the end of a hollow tube, and blowing it like a bubble to the required shape. The old laborious method involved a core of sand, mud, and other binding material fixed on the end of a tapering metal rod, baked, and then coated with molten glass. When the glass had cooled both rod and the core were removed. Glass blowing revolutionised glassmaking and ensured that many more articles could be produced.

Nowadays, a hollow steel tube, about four feet long, is used as the blow-iron, with a cronite nozzle end to prevent discolouring the glass it touches. The blow-iron is inserted through the mouth of the pot. By deftly rotating the nozzle on the surface of the molten glass, and skilfully judging the correct temperature and right amount of glass for the article to be made, the glassmaker withdraws the blow-iron and rolls the "gather" on a "marver"—a polished iron table. Marvering gives the glass its preliminary shaping and a cooler skin to contain the bubble as this is being blown into shape, either free-hand or with the aid of a mould. The shaping is achieved by such skilled manipulations as blowing, swinging, and blocking. Where necessary a stem and foot are added.

A small furnace known as a "glory hole" is used by the handmaking team at various stages of their work for re-heating.

The glass is then passed to a senior member of the team who makes the final forming after it has been fixed to a pontil rod (or "punty"), or in the case of lighter stemware to a "gadget" (a spring clip device), and after the glass has been knocked off the blow iron.

Few simple tools are used, not varying a great deal in many years—calipers for checking dimensions, wooden blocks for shaping, and sometimes shears to cut off the surplus glass. Pearwood, ideal for its durability and high surface finish is used in connection with shaping the feet of stemware.

Spring steel tools known as "pucellas" are used for pre-shaping stems, while special prepared carbon blocks fitted to hand held calipers are used for the final shaping.

The cast iron blow moulds are coated with charcoal dust or fine cork powder. It is difficult to convey in mere words the glasshouse scene—the individual skills of the craftsmen and the splendid teamwork which produces the "blank" drinking glass, jug, vase or decanter, ready for the decorator. Fortunately, there are now excellent facilities for visitors to witness the scene.

Terms used for members of the glassmaking teams vary from place to place. At Penicuik a "servitor" is the one who applies the stem and foot; the "footmaker" strangely enough is the one who blows the bowls; the "bit-gatherer" provides the servitor with small gobs of molten glass for adding the stems and feet, while the "taker-in" transports the final product to the "lehr" for annealing.

"Continental blower" is a term used to describe a blowing technique that originated from glassmakers who came from the Continent earlier this century.

Annealing is an essential part of glassmaking. If glass was not properly annealed, permanent strains would remain or be set up in the finished article, and the glass would be unable to withstand the decorating process and even normal usage without shattering.

In the "lehr", the annealing oven, glass is placed on a slowly moving conveyor, allowing the glass to cool from about 450°C to emerge from the lehr at room temperature, after a period of two to three hours. Larger articles are placed on static shelves in an oven, with the temperature adjusted as required for efficient annealing. All glasses are carefully checked for strain by using a polariscope. Those with flaws are rejected, broken, and used as cullet.

Various steps are taken to ensure that each article has a fine rim. The removal of the "overblow" by mechanical means after annealing leaves a rim which has to be flattened on a horizontal wheel, then bevelled inside and outside, and finally rounded slightly by heat. (Diamond impregnated tools on saw machines have now replaced the old laborious and costly techniques for removing excess glass from large pieces.)

The superior rim thus produced is characteristic of high quality British glass.

Cutting

The most widely used method of decorating crystal glass is known simply as "cutting", whereby the beauty of the glass is greatly enhanced. During the past hundred years Britain has become famed for its brilliant cut crystal glass.

Initially guide lines are painted on each article to be decorated, and within these simple markings the cutter works free-hand, gently pressing the glass against the revolving wheel.

In early days mitre cuts were achieved by using the edge of a flat stone wheel. Then a mitre edged wheel was introduced, thus simplifying the execution of this important type of cut. During the present century both stone and manufactured carborundum wheels have been used, some of the finest stone coming from Edinburgh's Craigleith quarries. It was necessary to cut patterns in two stages—the first cuts being done by "roughers". These "rough cuts" were then worked over by "smoothers" using finer wheels. Rounded edge and flat wheels are used for intaglio work and fluted patterns. Nowadays diamond impregnated wheels are used to complete the cutting at one stage in the majority of patterns, although some require the conventional roughing and smoothing cutting methods to achieve the necessary surface quality.

In all cases the wheels are fed by water, which acts as a lubricant while cutting is being done. The wheel speeds vary between 200 and 4,000 revolutions per minute depending on wheel diameter and width, and also type of the cutting.

Polishing

As mentioned previously, at the beginning of the 20th century polishing was done by wooden and brush wheels fed using putty powder, and pumice powder. During the 1920s acid polishing replaced this lengthy process in which hand polishing often took longer than the actual decoration. The former brilliance of the original surface is restored now by briefly dipping the decorated article into a mixture of concentrated hydrofluoric and sulphuric acids. This is a skilful operation, the operator having to make sure

35. Glasshouse, Penicuik, completed 1974. (Edinburgh Crystal)

that a high polish is achieved without impairing the sharpness of the cut facets. Control of the concentration of the two acids and the temperature, as well as the time of immersion, are vital factors in successful acid polishing.

The old lead lined vats are now replaced by those made of polypropolene. These contain the acids more efficiently, and sophisticated effluent treatment deals adequately with hazardous fumes and by-products created in this chemical process.

Engraving

Wheel engraving is an even more highly skilled craft. In this decorative technique a revolving copper wheel (ranging from the size of a pin head to 4″ diameter) fed by emery powder and oil, applied by the fingers of the engraver, can produce wonderful effects on glass—floral patterns, portrayal

F

of the human figure, coats of arms, emblems, and fine lettering. Another type of engraving using a diamond point to scratch or stipple a pattern, is not now used in the larger glassworks.

Edinburgh Crystal's Thistle service features engraving and fine cutting, and many commemorative pieces are fine examples of a craft which goes back to the Bohemian engravers of the 17th century.

Not only did Edinburgh Crystal have its own engravers working at Norton Park, but a number of other engravers such as the Millers did outside work for the firm. It is a sad fact that the older records of firms like Edinburgh Crystal have disappeared, and with them the names of craftsmen and the wages and payments they received.

During the present century engravers such as Mr Fred Lonie have upheld Edinburgh Crystal's reputation for fine quality engraved glassware.

Edinburgh district is famed for engravers such as Helen Monro (Mrs WES Turner), Alison Kinnaird, Alison Geissler, and Norman Orr—all at one time connected with Edinburgh College of Art and all of whom used Edinburgh Crystal blanks. It is interesting to learn that Mrs Geissler's grandfather, Alexander Garland, was an engraver at Norton Park during the late 19th century.

In the late 1960s Mr Orr stated that he had worked on articles from many parts of the world, but there was no glass to equal Edinburgh Crystal for the qualities he required for engraving.

Helen Monro, who founded the Glass Design Department at Edinburgh College of Art, and Mr E M Dinkel, Principal, (previously principal of the Stourbridge College of Art) were both Consultant Designers to Edinburgh Crystal.

Sand Etching

Sand etching, using a sand blasting technique, is becoming widely employed in the decoration of glass. Standard and fine grain manufactured abrasive "sands" are used according to the effect desired. The "sand" is projected through a stencil, produced from processes incorporating the photography of original art work, and screen printing. By varying the pressure, and a number of maskings, a lightly "powdered" or a deeper tone can be achieved.

Sand etching enables the finest detail to be reproduced on the glass surface more quickly, and larger quantities to be produced more economically.

Final Inspection

At the final inspection stage, glassware is graded, only first quality being marked with the Edinburgh Crystal trade-mark termed a "back stamp".

36. Cutting shop, Penicuik, completed 1968. (Edinburgh Crystal)

Small irregularities cannot be eliminated entirely from hand-made glass. No matter how skilled the craftsmen there are bound to be slight variations between similar articles. These should not be regarded as defects. Neither should "seeds" or "bubbles" be regarded as flaws. Although virtually all these are removed in the refining process, small isolated ones remain. Also when two pieces of glass are joined together during the making of an articles a small air bubble may be encased.

"Cords", slight differences in the refractive index, are also unavoidable in practice, and unless very pronounced, should not be regarded as defects. It is a matter of pride at Edinburgh Crystal that variations, seeds, bubbles, and cords are as minimal as is humanly possible, as are the mould, tool and shear marks which can sometimes be detected. All these are signs of genuine handmade glass.

When customers are made aware of the number of craftsmen and processes involved in crystal glassmaking, usually they no longer believe that this high quality product is too expensive.

6. Patterns Old and New

Thistle

It is only natural that producers of a wide range of fine Scottish glass should feature in their range a Thistle service. There is a continuous demand for Edinburgh Crystal's Thistle service from various parts of the world. It is one of the cornerstones of the firm's productions.

The thistle has been a Scottish symbol from the 17th century. A legend partly explains. When Stirling Castle was being attacked by Norsemen in the 8th century, hoping to steal silently on their intended victims, the invaders rashly decided to divest themselves of footwear. Fortunately for the Scots the enemy had made no allowance for the thistles through which they had to tread. It needs no strong imagination to picture the scene and realise why the Norsemen gave themselves away. It is a matter of no great importance that another version of the thistle legend sets the scene in North-West Scotland around the year 980AD when the Norsemen or Danes were attacking the Scottish clansmen. The procedure and result were the same! With the thistle symbol well established, James II, in 1687, founded the Most Ancient Order of Thistle.

Around 1895 the firm had introduced a liqueur set consisting of a thistle shaped decanter with six thistle shaped glasses (D325).

The Thistle Suite (pattern number H828) was revived during the 1920s and augmented from time to time with additional pieces. This new design was first produced as a whisky set comprising a quart decanter with lapidary cut stopper and six goblets. The decanter was similar in shape to the present wine decanter in the Thistle suite. During the late 1920s a full wine service was developed.

The service featured a cut diamond pattern around the centre, the neck and lower part of the decanter having cut flutes, and the upper part and stem of each glass a similar fluted pattern. An engraved thistle motif was included. A suite was presented to Edinburgh's Huntly House Museum.

Some of the service was given as a present to Princess Margaret on her marriage, from the Glasgow and Ayrshire Regiment. Lord Provost Brechin gave Thistle pattern decanters and glasses to the Mayor of Florence, Edinburgh's "twin" city.

Lochnagar (and another "Royal" pattern)

The feature of Lochnagar pattern, dating from Queen Victoria's reign, is a wide band of "Dutch diamonds" surmounted by a pattern of engraved vines.

For many years it has been the custom of the Corporation of Edinburgh to make a gift of crystal glassware to mark a royal wedding. King George V and Queen Mary were presented with a wine service by the city. Samples of this are in Huntly House Museum, and similar glasses had been supplied to Holyrood House.

On her marriage in 1960, Princess Margaret received a full service of 175 pieces. Completed in three weeks, these comprised port, sherry, claret and champagne glasses, tumblers, jugs, ice plates and decanters, and involved 20 craftsmen, some of whom took part in the production of glass presented to Princess Elizabeth (now Queen Elizabeth II), on her marriage in 1947. This was the E1290 pattern, featuring a design comprising long and short flutes.

Star of Edinburgh

The Star of Edinburgh remains another cornerstone of the Edinburgh Crystal range—a proud emblem of the City of its origin. Introduced in 1949 as an answer to critics, it was a breakaway into the field of simple clean cut design, featuring an elegant star symbolising the spirit of the glassmakers' art. Interestingly a star was depicted on 18th century glasses, thus the Star of Edinburgh is a modern interpretation of a Scottish emblem used in glass decoration for at least two centuries. By the 1960s this pattern, along with those of the Thistle and Lochnagar, had become the three most popular of all Edinburgh Crystal services. In 1982 a selection of this service was chosen for use on the American Presidential yacht USS *Sequoia*.

Iona

An elegant suite striving to reflect the history of the small but internationally known island with religious associations through the centuries. Now the community is a simple crofting one, but travellers from all over the world continue to visit the island because of its past alone.

Glenshee

The scenic grandeur of the Glenshee area, best seen from the 3059 ft Cairnwell mountain or from the Cairnwell Pass, Britain's highest main road pass, has inspired this classic suite.

Highland

To many the Highlands symbolise the real Scotland. Proud and independent, the Highlanders have their own culture, customs, and dress, with a background of some of Britain's finest scenery.

Sutherland

One of Britain's most northerly counties, but the "Southern land" of the early Norse settlers, Sutherland is becoming more popular amongst discerning visitors, who appreciate more and more its varied scenery, both coastal and inland, as well as its atmosphere of vast, empty and unspoiled countryside.

Appin

Also named after a Scottish region and reflecting Appin's rugged granite simplicity. Introduced in 1956, this pattern remains popular seemingly because of its dignity and clarity of form.

Lomond

The inspiration for the Lomond design derives from Scotland's most famous loch, renowned the world over for its outstanding beauty and romantic connotations.

Star of Edinburgh
1946

Iona 1981

Glenshee 1968

Highland
1974/1979

Sutherland
1981

Appin
1966

Lochnagar
1900

Lomond
1982

St. Giles
1977

37. Current and recent Edinburgh Crystal patterns.

38. Jacobite glasses reproductions.

39. The Star of Edinburgh.

40. From the current Thistle service.

41. "Breath of Scotland." The golfer.

42. "Caledonian Collection." Engraved illustration of salmon.

7. The Pattern Books

There are 14 substantial volumes of Edinburgh Crystal's pattern books preserved at Penicuik, providing an important and interesting record of Edinburgh & Leith Flint Glass from the late 1870s.

The following is a list of the volumes, with a selection of entries. Particularly noteworthy is volume L, mentioned later, containing drawings of reproductions of Jacobite glasses. Some of these are illustrated in this book.

Book One (Not lettered, but with some B and N numbers inserted much later)
Decanter. 32 point star. August 1 1877.
Tumbler. Richardson shape. March 28 1879. Samples sent to Pitcairn. New York. Some N numbers dated 1929, 1930.

This miscellaneous volume includes a series of mottos for bell goblets.
Dae as the lassies dae, say no an' tak it.
It's no lost what a freen gets.
Success to temperance, down with drink.
Freens like fiddle strings, mauna be screwed over ticht.
Cocktail glass—24.10.33.

"A" Pattern Book
This volume is not one of the earliest, dating from the 1920s.

A1	Goblet with knop and tears 1924.
A2	Opal twist stems (copies of Bristol Glass 1755 and 1760).
A4	A modern service with grapefruit, 13.11.30.
A27	Reproduction of old ginger jar and cover.

"B" Pattern Book
This book illustrates a number of skilfully made Venetian style glasses during the 1880s, also lighting ware of the period.

B57	Decanter with bird.
B124	Comport, Flint and Opal.
B180	Glass with pink frills, Venetian mould.

B326	Swan salt—double moulded.
B327	Swan cream. Venetian. Double moulded.
B328	Venetian cream. Sugar to match.
B330	Vase. Venetian. Flint.
B386	Glasses, purple, with green feet. Also one with green handle.
B393	Glass, crackled and threaded, leaf, green decoration.
B439–471	A series of threaded vases with applied mistletoe decoration.
B504	Water set—flint, turquoise, ruby.
B659–662	A vase with frill rim, cornucopia shape, on domed foot—flint, ruby, amber and opal.
B712	Small claret decanter and stopper. Ruby and amber square body moulded on B710.
B745 etc.	Moons. Obs (cured) and stained. Baird, Glasgow.
B749	Nelson moon. Engraved, etched and obs.
B751	Cup. Obs, cut, and etched.
B756	Globe. Stained sun flower.
B769	10/2/86—Cutter—Hambrey.
B772	Square bottle. Wilkes Dudley. No. 309.
B784	Spirit bottle. Wilkes Dudley. Cut Russian hobnail and prism.
B785	Large oval toilet tray 4/87.

"C" Pattern Book

C1	Water set. Complete 25/6 (1886?)—1900 27/–.
C10½	Polished engraving.
C11	Kaulfurs engraving.
C60	Sherbert as supplied to Parsons, Canada (1887).
C70 etc.	Decanter. Cut and engraved. Rock crystal.
C76	Toilet bottle. Cut and engraved. Rock crystal.
C407¾	Water set. Amber. Twist Goblet. Jug. Osler & Co. (the Birmingham firm).

"D" Pattern Book

This book, and the "C" book, show some extremely fine cut patterns.

D5	Wild roses. Etched by Guest Brothers (Stourbridge).
D26	Sent to Hampton & Sons, April 1892.

D30 Service of glass:
Sherrie *(sic)*. Port. Claret. Champagne. Liqueur. Custard. Jellie *(sic)*. Tumbler. Soda. Finger. Ice Plate. Qt. pt. and Claret Decanters. Carafe and cup. Ruby Hock.

D93 Service. Moulded and engraved rock crystal.

D353 Set of Spanish wines. Cut dia(mond) leg and star foot. Three fishes round and water. Cut to represent hammered glass.

"E" Pattern Book

E402 Highball tumbler supplied to Tiffany, New York.

E595 Ship decanter. Step cutting.

E698 Key border and two lines.

E1290 etc. Service of glass. Cut as sketch for Osler.
Typed list for Princess Elizabeth's wedding present.

"F" Pattern Book

F Qt. decanter. Old Waterford.

F105½ Admiralty 1910.

F167 Service of glass—etched brambles 29/6/10.

F237 Greenfield cutting only, pickle and top. (Greenfield was in charge of cutting shop.)

F810/R723 8″ soup plate supplied to Schmidt, Los Angeles.

"H" Pattern Book

H73 Hock. Flint 54/ doz.
    Blue 63/ doz.
    Puce 63/ doz.
    Ruby 63/ doz.
    Amber 63/ doz.

H724 Tudor Rose Suite.

H828 Thistle Suite. Jug on K122, 4 thistles and 6 leaves on each side.
12 flutes 23 rows diamonds, 24pt s.b. (star base) and beaded edge.

H1037 Twin oil bottle.

H1055 Supplied to Palfrey, Melbourne.

"K" Pattern Book

K5 Bell Goblet with motto "A wee deoch an dorus".

K58	(Repro.) 18th c. glass.
K59	(Repro.) Middle 18th c.
K60	(Repro.) Dutch late 18th and 19th c.
K62	Goblet 11⅜" engraved James II. Rose, leaves and buds.
K95	10" Vase. Blue and Opal.
K104	Quaich.
K238	Loud speaker and lamp (patented 3 May 1926).

"L" Pattern Book

Some of the finest of the one hundred "L" patterns are for reproductions of 18th century Jacobite glasses (see also K62). At the end of the sequence is the note "All these must have punty mark". Three examples are listed below:

L98	Wine glass. Young Pretender wearing bonnet fullfaced in Highland costume and wearing ribbon and star flanked by rose bud and thistle, inscribed "Audentior ibo" in ribbon. Owner (of original) says this glass was used by Prince Charlie at a Banquet given him by the Ladies of Edinburgh 1745.
L99	Goblet. Portrait Young Pretender in medallion in centre of an oak tree complete with stem, branches and leaves. Reverse side: Fiat over a star. Date 1760–70.
L100	Goblet. Date 1715–20. Portrait Young Pretender in round medallion surmounted by crown, below medallion: ribbon inscribed: Though He Fall He Shall Not be Utterly Cast Down For The Lord Upholdeth Him With His Hand

---

L312	Service of glass etched slanting "key" pattern.
L349	Candlestick. Specially done for Tiffany 30/5/27.
L795	10" Candlestick supplied to Jenkinson.
L812	Acid polished.
L8d8	14" Trumpet vase handmade by T. Webb & Sons.
L849	Four sizes of Vase/Dice Box made in Walsh Walsh mould.
L850	Service of glass for Thos. Webb & Sons. "They send pattern to work to, also their mould".
L854	Tall champagne. Sample to Fischer, Italy.

"M" Pattern Book

Several "M" patterns were supplied to Ford's, Edinburgh.

M29	Cocktail made out of claret mould. Supplied to Tozer Kemsley 12/12/32.
M31	Service—same shapes as K140 but wines calf leg (i.e. inverted baluster).
M33	Reserved to Jenners. Service as E112, but fluted leg instead of dabs.
M137	Engraved coaching scene.
M138	Engraved Huntsman in full cry. } as rubbing in engraving shop.

As supplied to Pitcairn, New York.

M357	12pt moulded star base.
M389	Coloured cased salad bowl, ruby, blue.
M418	Goblet sent to BET (British Empire Trades) Exhibition, Buenos Aires. Engraved bust of Prince of Wales in medallion surrounded by Roses, Thistles, etc., 3 feathers and Ich Dien above. HRH The Prince of Wales. In band below Patron on opposite side

Exposition Britanica

De

Arts et Industries

1931

(Lonie has rubbing in Engraving Shop.)

M434	8″ Cameo Fluer *(sic)* Vase (Ruby).
M435	9″ Salad bowl. Green, Blue, Amethyst, Ruby.
M450	Cameo Fleur vase on M16 shape. Stippled background. Blue, Green, Amethyst, Ruby, Amber.
M451	Cameo Fleur Tumbler vase.

N.B. A number of articles, e.g., Dice box vases, 9″ salad bowls, 10″ vases in above colours were decorated with cameo designs.

M496	Royal shapes. Stourbridge patterns No. 45244 for etching only. Sherry, Ports, Claret, Champagne, Royal tumbler.
M499	Lion's head prunt in each corner.
M631	Opal Swan (Black/Yellow eyes).
M792	Various items, made heavy for jewellers. Mitre cutting 90°. Celery, Jugs, Honey, Sugar, Tumbler, Bowl (sugar dated 14.6.32).

(Deeper cutting made possible by use of carborundum powder.)

M797 etc.	New samples. Lemonescent. Vases, grapefruit (also in blue).
M802	Tumbler vase. Lemonescent cameo decoration.

"P" Pattern Book

P11	Supplied to Shorter 6/1/32.
P32 etc.	Octagonal bowl, Blue, Tag design. Chrysolite bowl. Green bowl. (The above not polished.)
P56	Blank bowl on feet—made for Webb & Co., Manchester.
P84	Lamp and shade. Blue, Amber, Flint.
P107, 108	Sample blanks for Canadian Cut Glass Co. Ltd., Winnipeg.
P137	Service. Machine-cut diamond. Hand cut lacing.
P363	Qt. decanters, pt. decanters, claret decanters, liqueur decanter, bitter bottle, ice plates, supplied by Thos. Webb, Stourbridge.
P405	Glass bowl with peg only supplied to Betjemann & Son, London. Peg left bright and notched to fit ½" diameter brass tube.
P476	(Various items cut deep diamonds using carborundum) 9" salad bowl, bases, dish, biscuit barrel, honey, cream, sugar, and butter (1934).
P567	Spoon tray.
P642 etc.	Shorter's samples. Grapefruit, jelly, chutney.
P778	King George V and Queen Mary Silver Jubilee Cup 1910–1935.
P818	30/3/35 Wine blanks supplied to Hingley's, Stourbridge.
P820	Fittings (for scent spray) bought from Vale & Charles, 181 Hockley Street, Birmingham.
P909	Hock glass. Shows colours used—Blue, mauve, citreon *(sic)*, amber, green.

"R" Pattern Book

R1	Port blown from E & L 0919T mould. Sherry blown from Richardson's mould No. 168, 29.11.30. Claret blown from Richardson's mould No. 170. Champagne blown from Richardson's mould No. 171.

(There follows a number of items blown from Richardson's moulds. At this time Richardson's had been taken over by Webb's.)

R46	Opal shade.
R136	Bending corn (early carborundum cutting).
R137 etc.	Lamp. Travellers' sample. Sandblasted at Richardson's. Acid polished (5 sec. dip). Design put on after.
R141	LNER badged ware.
R707	Goblet. Air twist. 27/9/38.

(Mr Gay mentioned that about this time some exotic glass ware was being supplied to Schmidt, Beverley Hills.)

"T" Pattern Book

T1	Decanter. Walker & Hall. 18.4.39.
T33	Services for T. Eaton Co. Ltd. Sketched from "Kosta" glass. (Mr Sven Fogelberg, General Manager of Webb's Crystal, had been Managing Director of Kosta Glassworks, Sweden.)
T300	Amber vase. New sample dip mould. Festoon.
T301	Amber vase. New sample dip mould. Spotted.
T302	Amber vase. New sample dip mould. Diamonds.
T303	Amber vase. New sample dip mould. Optic.
T414 etc.	8″ vases; 2 American eagles, 2 camels, 2 kangaroos, koala bear, 2 elephants, lyre bird, seals, 3 penguins, 2 penguins, Indian Chief.
T408	(Tumbler vase) P320 shape. Scottish Industries Fair 28.8.49.
T444 etc.	Carver rest.
T562	Well shades for Osler. Made in wood moulds.
T569	Thistle tots. Samples to Webbs Crystal Glass Inc., New York.
T601	Three rows Vandyke splits. Open diamonds. (Emery powder used, for deep cuts.)
T707	Lager jug. Blank originally Webb's. June 1963.

INDEX

Numbers refer to pages: those in **bold** indicate
illustrations.